# CREATION

Martin Israel was born in Johannesburg where he qualified as a medical practitioner before emigrating to Britain to further his education. In parallel with his medical studies he became increasingly involved in psychological and spiritual investigation. This culminated in his ordination to the Anglican priesthood in 1975.

He teaches pathology at the Royal College of Surgeons of England, and is also priest-in-charge of the church of Holy Trinity with All Saints in London. He has an active ministry of counselling and healing, and conducts retreats all over the country.

Dr Israel has written a considerable number of books including *Gethsemane* and *The Dark Face of Reality* (published as Fount Paperbacks).

# CREATION

*The Consummation of
the World*

MARTIN ISRAEL

Collins
FOUNT PAPERBACKS

First published in Great Britain by
Fount Paperbacks, London
in 1989

Copyright © Martin Israel 1989

Phototypeset by Input Typesetting Ltd, London
Printed and bound in Great Britain by
William Collins Sons & Co. Ltd,
Glasgow

You should try your hardest to supplement your faith with virtue, virtue with knowledge, knowledge with self-control, self-control with fortitude, fortitude with piety, piety with brotherly kindness, and brotherly kindness with love.

*2 Peter 1: 5–7*

# CONTENTS

*Prologue*                                    9

1 Let There Be Light                         11
2 Creation and Evolution                     27
3 The Creation of Humanity                   41
4 Humanity Come of Age                       57
5 The Springs of Human Creativity            70
6 Man and Nature                             85
7 The Making of a Person                    103
8 The Priesthood of Humanity                118
9 The Consummation of All Things            134

# PROLOGUE

To embark on a short account of the creative process from the beginning of the world to our present day is no easy matter. It requires sufficient factual knowledge to make the venture credible, and also a deeper spiritual awareness to invest that knowledge with significance that goes beyond the apparent finality of mortality to the concept of fulfilment in life eternal. The conflict between science and religion has been sad, for each has something vital to give the other: truth on the one hand and vision on the other. Where there is no vision, the people break loose (Proverbs 29:18), but the vision must come from a person with lawful authority. This authority comes with obedience to an ongoing tradition, whether civil or religious, and also the intellectual capacity to receive and analyse new data that are constantly impinging upon us all.

In this book I have drawn upon the knowledge of various authorities. Amongst those especially of note are *Science and Creation* by John Polkinghorne, which has instructed me in physics and cosmology; *Origins* by Richard E. Leakey and Roger Lewin as well as *The Making of Mankind* by Richard E. Leakey, both invaluable sources of information about biological evolution and anthropology; *Back from the Brink* by

Guy Mountford, an important account of success in wildlife conservation; *Latin America: a Short History* by George Camacho and *Everyday Life of the Incas* by Ann Kendall, which have given me details about the aboriginal inhabitants of Central and South America; *The Hutchinson Encyclopedia of Living Faiths*, edited originally by R. C. Zaehner; *A New Science of Life: The Hypothesis of Formative Causation* and its successor *The Presence of the Past* by Rupert Sheldrake, which discuss the interesting concept of "morphic resonance" as part of the evolutionary process; and finally *Chaos* by James Gleick, the making of a new science.

I would finally like to thank my parents and mentors who have made it possible for me to appreciate all this knowledge through the education they afforded me, culminating both in my medical profession and my work as a Christian priest.

# 1

# Let There Be Light

We read in the Genesis story that when God made heaven and earth, the earth was without form and void, with darkness over the face of the abyss, and a mighty wind that swept over the surface of the waters. God said, "Let there be light", and there was light; and God saw that the light was good. Though the scientific understanding of the origin of the universe far exceeds this allegorical account of creation, the insight contained in it, that of a transcendent creator who wills a creation into existence by the power of his mighty word, is eternally valid. It is estimated that the universe is about 15,000 million years old, and that it came into creation following a mighty explosion in which the elementary particles of matter evolved out of pure energy. These particles – the gluon, the quark (which together constitute the proton) and the electron – are believed to be the building-blocks of the universe, the microcosm, as it were, reflected in the macrocosm of the entire creation. This "big bang" theory of the origin of the universe is now accepted as the most likely mechanism of creation by cosmologists, since re-echoing background cosmic radiation still persists as an aftermath of the great explosive event.

But what existed before this dramatic event? To the person aware of spiritual reality, the answer is plain: God alone, the transcendent Creator, for in the Deity, whose nature cannot be delineated but whose emergent qualities lie revealed in his intrinsic energies that are beyond creation while the very foundation of it, there is a source of unceasing creativity. The uncreated is the ceaseless creator of the universe. At a certain juncture he willed the universe, but where could space be found since the divine presence is infinite as well as eternal? It is traditionally accepted that God creates form out of nothing (2 Maccabees 7:28 is a classic statement of this theme). It is of interest that the speculation of gnostics was the first to penetrate the mechanism. Thus the sixteenth-century messianic Kabbalist Isaac Luria explained the existence of the universe in terms of a willed contraction, or shrinkage (the Hebrew word is *tsim-tsum*), in God, who thereby afforded space of himself for the creation of something independent of him while being simultaneously of his very essence. Gershom G. Scholem in his magisterial work *Major Trends in Jewish Mysticism* finds a similar explanation of the universe in the writing of the second-century gnostic thinker Basilides and in the gnostic *Book of the Great Logos*, preserved through Coptic translation. Both Luria and the gnostics believed that God had left an essence of himself in the space he provided for independent creation to occur, comparable with the residue of oil or wine in a bottle after the contents have been poured out, or the fragrance of a sweetly smelling unguent remaining in a bowl emptied with the greatest possible care. Whatever may be the mechanism, the courtesy and loving kindness of a Creator who fashions unceasingly while providing his creatures with a freedom to explore the universe, tracing their own paths through its complexity, is the very foundation of the process of evolution. From the elementary particles of physics are derived the more complex elements and compounds of chemistry and ultimately the spiralling nucleic acids that are the very backbone of life itself. How this process of steady evolution progressed through the aeons is still not understood, but in due course living creatures arose that could respond to the milieu around no less than within themselves. Eventually came the great moment when they could co-operate purposefully in the continuous work of the Deity. This was the time of human emergence.

Creation in form includes within its process both the eternal order of God and the built-in capacity for disorder that is the basis of evolution. Just as a well-mannered youth, schooled in the edifying environment of his home, has in due course to reach beyond the mantle of imposed discipline and learn to mix in a far less scrupulous world, so all that lives is bound to compete for its existence in a domain where the fittest alone survive. If the individual fails to adapt he will inevitably perish, but if he follows the blind rapacity of the masses, he is liable to be crushed to death. It is his ability to stand out by virtue of his intrinsic integrity that will ensure not only his survival but also his contribution to the welfare of the whole community; indeed, life flourishes most effectively in the type of circumstance where there is underlying order but of such an openness that the individual may actualize his own unique potentiality in freedom while in the context of the whole community. If he is outstanding in some quality he may disturb the current order. But in due course this change becomes the pattern of a higher order, in turn challenged by fresh insights.

The formless void that followed the withdrawal of the divine presence is traditionally called chaos. The concept has been broadened to embrace the great deep of primordial matter, which in terms of modern physics is composed of the elementary particles that were created when the uncreated energies of God exploded at his command to form the foundation of the universe. Nowadays we associate chaos with a state of utter confusion wrought by climatic catastrophe or human lawlessness, but in fact the original mass of primordial matter was orderly in arrangement and of immense fecundity: as the Genesis narrative puts it, "God saw that it was good". Our own planet is a mere speck in the vastness of a universe whose span, measured in light years, is beyond the grasp of most of us.

And yet the universe itself is only part of an infinitely more extensive realm of non-material essence in which pure thought is aligned to psychic entities and spiritual consciousness. St Paul in Ephesians 6: 10–12 speaks about life's great battle being not so much against human agencies as cosmic powers, the authorities and potentates of this realm's dark recesses, the superhuman forces of evil in the heavens. This dramatic warning presents the forbidding side of the picture, but it is balanced by an array of beneficent forces allied to the development of life and the growth of the person. These include the noetic, or intellectual, realm of mathematical truth, the moral dimension of justice and compassion that enables civilization to proceed, and the vast communion of unseen agents that influence the conduct of the universe. These include the angelic hierarchy and the souls of the departed – and possibly those coming into incarnation if we may consider spiritual pre-existence as a serious option. There is also the nebulous field of psychical phenomena whose study defines the controversial discipline of parapsychology.

When the universe came into being, time commenced and space showed itself; in the time/space universe, growth takes place and the rational creature thrives under its discipline. By contrast the vast intermediate, non-material realm lies outside the limits of time and space. It existed before the creation as described in the Bible. It therefore transcends the time and space that define our experience of earthly life. Nevertheless, this mental/psychic/spiritual realm, determining so much of our day-to-day response to the world we inhabit, is not to be identified with the Deity. He created both heaven and earth, heaven in this context being identified with the non-material spiritual world on whose action the well-being of the universe depends. When then was this intermediate spiritual realm created? To this question a tangible answer seems well nigh impossible, since time, as we know it, does not enter the matter. Nevertheless, the non-material realm presumably had its own coming to birth into universal reality where it apparently fully reflected the mind of the Creator. The existence of the dark forces in its midst suggests a fall before the birth of the universe, but more we cannot say. The spiritual world gives form to the material creation, while the universe brings the spiritual dimension into tangible action.

Another mystery is the cause of creation. Why did God perform the stupendous feat of making the universe? Inasmuch as the Deity is complete in itself, it requires nothing external for its own integrity. The trinitarian scheme of orthodox Christianity asserts a complete loving relationship between Father and Son with the Holy Spirit as a mediator of that love. Therefore the three hypostases, or persons of the Godhead, are in a state of eternal perfection of being, both individually and together. However, the proof of love is its desire to share its riches; as long as a relationship is withdrawn and secreted, however strong the devotion of the parties to one another, the operating force is a fear of separation. Love that is real never counts the cost, for the Spirit of God rules the heart and will never be at peace until it has brought all creatures home. Thus St Paul can see that suffering itself strengthens us in the hope of the divine splendour that is to be ours. He goes on to reflect that such a hope is no mockery, because God's love has flooded our inmost heart through the Holy Spirit he has given us (Romans 5:3–5).

I doubt whether anyone who has not suffered grievously can know the exultation of true love as opposed to well-meaning goodwill. We tend to be most generous when the things we prize most are no longer ours; having nothing material we are aware of our unadorned integrity, and this we can give freely to others. The more we give, the greater is the inner radiance. This radiance is the Holy Spirit within us, and when God creates the cosmos (this is the universe and the intermediate mental/psychic/spiritual realm), it is a manifestation of his outpouring love. A loving human family will have little difficulty in bringing a stranger home. The hazards inherent in such a foolhardy venture will scarcely enter their minds, whereas a more practically orientated group will stare the possible consequences full in the face and act with sensible circumspection. And who can blame them? The introduction of an unknown member may so easily disrupt the present equilibrium and create havoc. The lesson is never to embark on such an enterprise except in a spirit of sacrifice. The consequences are the only reward: the more that is anticipated, the greater is the disappointment liable to be. But when there is love, the less is any reward of consequence. God created the cosmos because of his outflowing love. Another way of stating this is to affirm the essential divine creativity, for such creativity is always loving. However, the creativity bestowed on the rational creature, divine in origin as it is, tends to be soiled by covetousness and so may reveal a destructive tendency.

Love takes infinite pains in all it creates, but is able to release the creature to carry on its own life. It therefore follows that innumerable variations of form may follow the divine creative act. Some experiments will be successful while others may fail to meet the exigencies of the present moment and be squeezed out of existence. Once creation has been effected, the creature's free will determines its fate. God does not simply step in to put everything in order. He is not a *deus ex machina*, an external power that comes in the nick of time to solve a difficulty and put everything right. He is also not a demiurge, merely a creator of the universe whose activity is limited to it. On the contrary, he is outside the created order but is unceasingly concerned in its welfare. His energies sustain the universe, and are at the disposal of his creatures in their toil of survival, procreation and participation in the maintenance of the world. The human, with his rational capacity, has a special privilege and responsibility in this participation, but everything that lives has its own part to play in sustaining the natural environment.

Creation can never cease except by divine decree. If this were to occur, it would imply a cessation of

God's love. The consummation of all things probably will see an end of the material creation, but then a new world will surely unfold before the Creator's loving care. The vision contained in Revelation 21 gives some indication of what this would mean.

The creation narrative of Genesis 1 and 2 gives a somewhat impersonal picture of God's activity. He is, in fact, intimately involved in his handiwork, like an artist. But whereas an artist can erase his production, God, by his gift of free will, has abdicated his immediate control over his creation, which is henceforth at liberty to use the divine gift, the power of the Holy Spirit, according to its own desires. When the full implication of this dawns on us, it becomes less intolerable that there should be disasters involving vast planetary systems no less than disruptions of our own environment: the whole created universe groans in all its parts as if in the pangs of childbirth (Romans 8:22). It has to attain its own form, to work out its own salvation "in fear and trembling" (Philippians 2:12), and here the human component can play a very important part, at least in our corner of the world. The universe is, of course, very much more than our small planet, and evolution involves the entire universe and not only our tiny part in it. We inhabit a geologically and climatically unstable planet, growing in the creative process, and we cannot assume that all will automatically go well with us. There are, for example, areas of the earth that are especially liable to earthquakes, volcanoes, floods, hurricanes, or droughts. It might be that part of the human contribution to the world lies not only in ameliorating these disasters by modern scientific methods but also in calming the elements by living peacefully and praying regularly. It is not outside the bounds of possibility that adverse human emotions have a climatic effect, while a calming of the human might leave its impress on the elements. Certainly prayer often settles adverse weather conditions. There are mysteries in creation more accessible to psychic communion than intellectual analysis, remembering always that both modes lie within the scope of the human spirit.

According to the Genesis story everything God created was fundamentally good. Modern theoretical physics stresses both the order inherent in the disposition of the elementary particles from which the universe was fashioned and their simultaneous unpredictability. The random nature of particle movement is part of the creative process whereby new combinations may constantly occur that alter the very rhythm of existence, while at the same time stabilizing it for the new demands that are to be made on it. Everything God created may well have been good, but there seems to be room for improvement; in other words, perfection is of a different order to goodness. The mechanism of the creative process is so well grounded that room is made for new possi-bilities to emerge in the course of its development. The end of the process is the spiritualization of our secular endeavour, so that the universe and the inter-mediate mental/psychic/spiritual realm can function as a composite whole. Therefore the goodness of creation that the biblical writer declares may be identified with the most favourable function a particular creature subserves at a given time. But there is always room for growth.

In his essay on *Compensation* R. W. Emerson made an important observation: there is a crack in everything God has made. To the fanatical moralist this crack is a flaw in construction that leads inevitably to the creature's destruction unless he is "saved" by God. However, to the rather less dogmatic experimentalist, whether in scientific research or in practical living, the crack is a means of growth, a way of expansion of the personality to new experiences. The very imperfection of the natural order provides the key to a more developed understanding of reality than the surface judgements so often given by those of little self-knowledge. He who has suffered long may be able to bear another's pain, whereas the untested individual will scarcely be able to comprehend his neighbour's difficulties, let alone give any intimate help. It may well be a pathetic fallacy to attribute such an understanding to the other animals, but it is certainly true of creation's masterpiece, the human who has been given charge over the remainder of the world's created order. In the creation story Adam and Eve live in such perfect harmony with the world around them that they have little self-awareness or thanks for the bliss that encompasses them. They are comparable to unborn children in the safety of the mother's womb or small children enjoying the undisturbed happiness of a loving family. Only when they are sent out into the more rigorous world of school and later competitive employment do they discover deeper aspects of themselves. They yearn for the past security while steeling themselves against the constant test of adverse circumstances that is the fruit of independence. Soon the onward thrust all but obliterates the memories of happy childhood. The final test is the preservation of childlike innocence in the adult world of fierce endeavour and dark treachery.

In the Genesis story Adam and Eve were unable to contain their yearning for power, and they excluded themselves from a loving relationship with the Creator. Nevertheless, the hard journey ahead saw the beginning of self-awareness and growth into adulthood. It is the perennial journey of the creature to independent progress in the world that God in his infinite love has prepared for him, his rejection of the divine grace, and his suffering. Painful as it may be for creature and God alike, it is the only way forward to proficiency. We please God most when we depend least on his help. In that state of true maturity we are in a relationship with him such that we work together as partners in the constant maintenance of the world. We are also able to apply new concepts that come to us from the inspiration of the Holy Spirit. In this way we can effect new developments that play their part in changing the face of the world: stasis is death, whereas progress is life. In the Parable of the Prodigal Son, the father shows great love in letting his headstrong son go, well aware as he must have been of the mess in front of him, and suffering all the pains of his ungrateful child. This love is as profound as the welcome he gave to the scapegrace when he returned destitute and humiliated. Love and joy come from a common source, and in their midst there is peace. None of these three depend on good fortune; they are manifestations of the eternal presence of God. Indeed, they render worldly prosperity trivial. It is in this frame of mind that creation proceeds most productively, for then there is no emotional conflict to interfere with the flow of the Holy Spirit, who is the giver of all inspiration.

When there is emotional disharmony the spiritual flow is impeded, if not stopped, but even in such an extremity there may be a blessing. When the flow is later restored after emotional equilibrium is attained, the experience of pain may open up previously unexplored paths of speculation. In this way an environment may be provided for a new creation to emerge. Nothing is ultimately lost in the creative love of God. The entire body of the universe is capable of resurrection, and it is the human privilege to promote this great undertaking.

I believe that when God created the universe, the inhabitants of the mental/psychic/spiritual realm gave a loud cheer. One remembers God's self-disclosure to Job (38:4–7), "Where were you when I laid the earth's foundations? Tell me, if you know and understand. Who settled its dimensions? Surely you should know. Who stretched his measuring-line over it? On what do its supporting pillars rest? Who set its corner-stone in place, when the morning stars sung together and all the sons of God shouted aloud?" Whenever the creative ray of divine light touches the void and brings form out of emptiness, a paean of joy sounds forth from the cosmos. Not only do the heavenly hosts proclaim their praise, but even the elementary particles, by their very existence, add their share to the general rejoicing. And when life itself shows forth, the acclaim is tumultuous.

The creation was God's great experiment. He himself did not and indeed does not know the final result. Free will cannot be tempered by divine intervention and still remain free. Nevertheless, God is in ultimate control since the cosmos is his creation. His love, which brought forth the world out of nothing but his own sacrifice, will never fail. Despite the independence of his creatures, from the random movements of elementary particles and their accompanying forces to the vicissitudes of living forms in a universe that is constantly changing as it undergoes further creation, he retains over-all charge of phenomena.

The means of control are the laws by which the universe is governed. On the physical level there are, for instance, the law of gravity and the laws of thermodynamics. Even more elementary and subtle is the theory of relativity which renders meaningless the concept of an instantaneously defined state of the world, while quantum mechanics requires that the state is in any case not observable. The laws of life require the organism's protection and nutrition as well as the needs of procreation, while the laws contingent on human relationships embrace a code of morality summed up in the Judeo-Christian Ten Commandments and similar injunctions contained in the world's other great religious traditions. Only on the foundation of law can life progress and its potentialities unfold. Variation can be held in creative tension with the established norm, while progress is balanced with tradition. Finally, it is not inconceivable that biological laws can themselves evolve. Nothing in the universe is static, and an advanced creature working in collaboration with the Holy Spirit might conceivably influence the form of life as we at present know it.

We considered the concept of chaos earlier on as the fundamental mass of primordial matter from which the universe was fashioned and also a state of utter confusion. Currently a new science has been created which is called "chaos theory". It examines the random nature of many natural processes that give the superficial impression of order; yet underneath, a more mysterious type of order prevails. It does indeed appear as if the accepted laws of nature are statements of approximations rather than rigid unchanging facts. The enormous scope for individual and communal development in the world is indeed a proof of the Creator's respect for the creatures that evolve from the potentialities of existence that have been prepared for them.

# 2

# Creation and Evolution

It is estimated that the earth came into being as part of our solar system some 4500 million years ago. It took another 1000 million years for conditions to have cooled sufficiently for life to emerge. A living organism, in contrast with inert matter, can respond creatively to its environment and has the capacity to procreate. The creature is endowed with some instinct of identity that strives for survival, an attitude that becomes especially dominant when powers of sense perception develop.

The basis of life still eludes scientific explanation even if its essential chemical determinant, deoxyribonucleic acid (DNA), is now well known and its genetic propensities become increasingly accurately mapped out. Life is response and growth; once life ceases, the organism becomes inert and soon tends to disintegrate. In Christian thought the Holy Spirit of God is described as the Lord, the giver of life. He animates all living forms, but they cannot acknowledge their source of existence until the human being evolves as nature's masterpiece of matter and spirit.

If God has emptied himself to make space for the material universe, how can he be present in a realm he has purposely left under his creature's control? How can the transcendent Deity be also immanent in even the meanest of his creatures without taking control and predetermining their mode of development? Too transcendent a God can become as remote as an absentee landlord, whereas too immanent a God can be bound up with his creatures to the extent of their becoming mere ciphers under his control. Alternatively, they may become merely manifestations of their creator, a state moving towards pantheism, in which nature is identified with God. Such a deity becomes as otiose a category as a remotely transcendent one. Like all mystical logic, the answer lies in the realm of *both/and* or *neither/nor* rather than the rational *either/or*. Luria's concept of a trace of the Deity being present in his creation, helpful for me personally, leads to the concept of panentheism, in which the divine essence pervades his creation. But the concept if taken to an extreme position can, like pantheism, pre-empt the creature's independence. As far as I have been allowed to see, the divine essence is a gift to the creature, which may either be accepted or rejected. One gift that is fundamental and unsolicited is that of life itself, but its use depends on the creature. The more primitive forms are carried along by their environment, but, as reason dawns, so does the capacity to choose come into its own and the will shows itself. I accept St Augustine's assessment of the human condition as one of inner restlessness until man rests in God. This inner knowledge is a direct communion with the Deity, and it is substantiated through the realm of mental communication as well as the labile matter of the universe.

Between 3000 and 500 million years ago various invertebrates made their appearance: blue-green algae followed by marine sponges and later by molluscs. By this time other types of algae were abundant, including those involved in building reefs. About 500 million years ago fishes appeared, and the first land creatures descended from them, the amphibians, saw the light of day some 400 million years ago. At about the same time the first insects appeared. The reptiles emerged 50 million years later. Meanwhile the first land plants, followed by the early seed plants, had established themselves, soon to be succeeded by the gymnosperms (plants with seeds unprotected by a surrounding vessel); about 270 million years ago coniferous trees evolved from them. At about this time mammal-like reptiles appeared which about 220 million years ago evolved into the fabulous dinosaurs. These prevailed until about 66 million years ago when they suddenly became extinct. The first mammals were probably contemporaneous with the dinosaurs, but they were able to survive. The first birds appeared about 135 million years ago. As the dinosaurs disappeared, so the more recognisable modern mammals thrived and spread over the world's surface. At that time the primate order first evolved.

Meanwhile the angiosperms, the flowering plants, appeared. These prevail in all but the coldest climates. The earth's crust was also undergoing dramatic changes. The supercontinent called Pangaea had begun to break up into the continents familiar to us; South America separated from the African mainland, and later the Alpine and Himalayan mountain systems formed. The climate cooled, and there were major ice ages between one and two million years ago (as well as more recently) alternating with warmer interglacial periods.

This information is readily available in specialist textbooks. Some, like the existence of Pangaea, is a hypothesis accepted by most geologists. The study of fossil remains by palaentologists has cast light on the origin and development of our small world, while the archaeologist's study of prehistoric antiquities has shed light on the more recent of our ancestors' way of life. What we see is a focus of matter evolving through vast aeons of time, being the source of innumerable biological experiments while its own substance groans under the whiplash of cosmic change. There is no predetermined pattern; chance apparently governs all, and yet as Gerard Manley Hopkins put it so beautifully in *God's Grandeur*:

And for all this, nature is never spent;
There lives the dearest freshness deep down things;
And though the last lights off the black West went
Oh, morning, at the brown brink eastward, springs –
Because the Holy Ghost over the bent

World broods with warm breast and with ah!
bright wings.

These thoughts fit in especially well with the human
vandalisation of the environment, but there are also
deeper undertones of the "whole creation groaning
in all its parts as if in the pangs of childbirth"
(Romans 8:22). The human adds his quota of pain to
the world, but suffering is an intrinsic part of all
growth to proficiency, even of so apparently inert a
substance as the matter that composes the world.
This is composed ultimately of elementary particles,
the gluon, quark and electron. All living things par-
take of the world's vulnerability, and none can claim
a special concession or dispensation from the unpredictability of cosmic phenomena that rock our little
home from time to time.

The order of primates probably first appeared 70
million years ago; it is divided into two main subor-
ders, the prosimians, small creatures that include the
mouse lemur, and the larger monkeys and apes. The
ape family includes the orang-utan, gorilla, chimpanzee and the human. The apes emerged about 45
million years ago, and the human species and the
contemporary great apes had common, fairly
immediate ancestors. Some 10 to 16 million years ago
there lived ape-like creatures who were the common
ancestral stock of the whole family. The Asian apes,
the orang-utans, diverged during this period. The
bulk, however, lived in Africa where the human was
to emerge. The gorilla diverged 8 to 10 million years

31

ago, followed by man's nearest relative, the chimpanzee, between 5 and 8 million years ago. The prehuman line continued until 2.5 to 2 million years ago, when the genus *Homo* broke away from the common ancestor, who apparently became more robust but lacked the brain power of the human, and subsequently disappeared from the face of the earth.

The momentous change that accompanied the appearance of *Homo* was the adoption of the erect posture, so that the forelimbs could develop into hands which could fashion tools in a systematic and culturally transmissible way. Thus *Homo habilis* (toolmaking man) emerged. There was a progressive increase in size and complexity of the brain, and there is now evidence that this early human of two million years ago had a spoken language (this has been deduced by the complexity of the brain structure as made evident in extant skulls with well-defined areas anatomically associated with speech similar to those found in contemporary humans). *Homo habilis* migrated to Asia from 1.8 to 1.5 million years ago, and this was closely followed by the transition to *Homo erectus*. Somewhere between 1.3 and 0.5 million years ago the control of fire was achieved, and from 750,000 to 250,000 years ago our own species, *Homo sapiens*, emerged. Between 100,000 and 25,000 years ago modern human culture was born.

The triumphal emergence and durability of the human species has been closely related to its intellectual ability. It is the only group that can adapt to a wide variety of terrestrial and climatic conditions.

Indeed, we can bend nature to suit ourselves, although in the end our versatility may bring forth a bitter harvest of destruction. Nevertheless, the biblical narrative and modern evolutionary theory agree in putting man at the top of the pyramid of animal development, at least as regards intelligence and therefore power over the remainder of creation in our small planet. Interestingly, the Bible traces the results of human disobedience to God in a progressive alienation from the animal creation. At first Adam and Eve feed on all the plants that bear seed everywhere on earth and every tree bearing fruit that yields seed, while the green plants are given to the lesser animals (Genesis 1:29–30). There is peace and harmony between man and animals. After the Fall there is first the terrible murder of Abel by Cain, fratricidal strife typical of human history, and then, after the Flood that destroys all creation other than Noah and his household, a new covenant proclaimed by God: the fear and dread of mankind shall fall upon all wild animals on earth, on all birds of heaven, on everything that moves upon the ground and all the fish in the sea; all are given into man's hands, and every creature that lives and moves is to be his food. The human moves from a harmless vegetarian mode of diet to unrestricted meat eating, except that flesh with blood (life) in it is forbidden (Genesis 9:2–4). The time of strife between man and animals has come, and will continue until the Spirit of God fully infuses the human spirit, when compassion and love triumph over gluttony and covetousness. The first eleven chapters of Genesis are unwisely seen in a limited historical perspective. They speak of eternal spiritual truth depicted allegorically and in parable, as indeed do all authentic spiritual teaching and all spiritually interpreted historical events. The end of the eleventh chapter merges slowly into the story of the patriarch Abraham, the first palpably historical character in the Bible.

The mode of evolution was described by Charles Darwin and Alfred Russel Wallace as "natural selection", depicted popularly as the survival of the fittest of a species, especially in times of privation when the common herd are liable to go to the wall. Darwin, from his detailed studies during his voyage on the *Beagle*, came to the conclusion that species themselves are not immutable but are capable of transformation, a far cry from the "creationism" implicit in the scriptural account of God making animals appear spontaneously in the course of a short period of time. Darwin's visit to the Galapagos Islands, a remote Pacific archipelago some hundreds of miles west of Ecuador, was especially seminal to his grasp of species development: each island seemed to have its own finch, sometimes even more than one according to the local environment, and yet all these birds clearly came from a common stock. In fact, Darwin's and Wallace's final theory had been preceded by the work of Erasmus Darwin, Charles' grandfather, the eminent geologist Charles Lyall, whose study of fossils showed him that the earth was a planet of great antiquity, and Jean Baptiste de Lamarck, who had brought out a prior theory of evolution that accepted the inheritance of acquired characteristics, a view at complete variance with subsequent research except in the case of some bacteria.

It was the science of genetics, pioneered by Gregor Mendel, that put evolutionary theory in a rational framework. Each organism has a pair of factors called genes, one from each parent, that control the appearance of a given characteristic. Usually one gene product dominates over the other, which then may be hidden, but sometimes both products are manifest. The genes are contained in the DNA of each individual cell nucleus in bodies called chromosomes, but it is the sex cells, the ova and spermatozoa, that are especially important in heredity, for by their fusion a new individual is born. These sex cells have half the number of chromosomes of the other body cells; when they fuse, a zygote, the unicellular form of a new individual, is formed. It rapidly divides and grows to form the organs and parts that characterize the mature organism. There is a random assortment of maternal and paternal chromosomes in each ovum and spermatozoon: we all bear points of clear resemblance to our parents, but there are also points of departure. Some genes remain unexpressed in a parent which subsequently manifest themselves in the offspring. Furthermore, a gene may undergo a random change, or mutation, during the processes of cell division prior to the final formation of the ovum or spermatozoon. This mutation may affect the individual himself, and will be inherited by any subsequent offspring. If the effect is baneful, the embryo may die or be born severely diseased, but if it is less severe, the individual will survive and transmit the gene with its effects to his progeny. The harmful genes fall under the inspection and management of the medical profession. Some mutated genes may be less dangerous and more beneficial, even helping the individual to cope in an indifferent environment. The progeny will then have the advantage over their peers, soon supplanting them to become the dominant group.

The classical Darwinian view, amplified by the neo-Darwinism that has followed genetic knowledge, sees evolutionary innovations as essentially the result of the accumulation of many slight modifications, the consequence of numerous mutations. But much controversy prevails. Some workers hold that many of the most important evolutionary events have arisen in single steps due to major mutations: a theory of "macromutations" as opposed to the usual one of "micromutations". This would tend to recognize the possibility of genetic forms arising spontaneously. It is, of course, possible that the two mechanisms could both occur in the course of evolution. Yet another approach envisages evolution as rather more than merely a sequel to chemical changes in the DNA molecule affecting one or more genes. It attributes the primary development of an organism to a non-material morphogenetic field arising from the mental/psychic/spiritual realm. Such a field would then determine the organism's form, which its genes then proceed to execute by virtue of their fundamental property of implementing the formation of proteins through the second nucleic acid of the cell, termed ribonucleic acid (RNA). Proteins are the basic building blocks of living organisms.

Such a mechanism meets with scant respect from most scientists, who not surprisingly prefer a thoroughgoing material explanation for all biological processes, since these are then immediately tractable to reason and control. Anything suggesting "vitalism" (the doctrine that life originates in a vital principle distinct from chemical and other physical forces) is taboo in traditional scientific thought, a prejudice not entirely to be dismissed, as the concept can let in a host of superstitions when placed in the wrong hands. Nevertheless, our lives do bear the impress of factors that reach beyond common reason, and these are constantly impinging upon them. Indeed, life itself is a mystery that cannot satisfactorily be reduced to purely material categories.

A current hypothesis that is arousing some interest is that of "causative formation", which postulates a series of "morphic fields" around each organism. These fields not only determine the form of the organism and its various parts but also have the property of inheriting present data to pass on to the organism's progeny. It is certainly difficult to envisage a field that bears memory sufficient to instruct future members of the same species, but it is the "morphic resonance" among those members (whether plant or animal) that is the means by which information, whether behavioural or evolutionary, is transmitted in a psychic milieu. The fields not only direct development but are also capable of evolution according to the environmental exigencies that may later confront the organism, so that there is a constant interplay between morphic field and organism. At present the hypothesis awaits experimental substantiation and rests on circumstantial evidence, but its very existence emphasizes the inadequacy of materialistic dogma in solving the mystery of life and evolution at least to the more spiritually aware person.

When the marvel of the creation of the universe is considered, we do well to remember, as astronomers tell us, that our small planet revolves around the sun, which is only one of ten thousand million stars in our galaxy, which, in turn, is only one of the millions of galaxies that make up the universe. Whether there is life elsewhere in the universe we do not know, but there seems to be no obvious reason why it should not be so. It is by no means unlikely that the microcosm, our solar system, is representative of the macrocosm, and what we are enabled to know of it, of which our earth is a small part, may be not unreasonably extended to regions beyond our present grasp yet part of the one creation. Though our minds may not be able to deal with the vast scale of the universe expressed numerically, we have an imagination that can travel beyond finite quantities to embrace an infinity which is greater than any sum of numbers that we could imagine. Thought, being instantaneous, travels faster than the speed of light. It can also comprehend the totality of the universe in a sweep that puts all finite measurement in its place as simply one mode of coming to terms with the inconceivable.

On the other hand, life on earth is intimately related to the material structure of the planet and other planets also. For instance, there is some evidence that the earth was struck by a large meteorite 66 million years ago, and it is possible that the sudden extinction of the dinosaurs was related to this event. It might have happened that the dense layer of dust from the meteorite blocked the sun's rays over part of the earth's surface, so interfering with photosynthesis, the process by which the energy of sunlight is used by the chlorophyll of green plants to build up carbohydrates from carbon dioxide and water. And so the dinosaurs may have starved to death. Two primitive marine reptiles, the ichthyosaurus and the plesiosaurus, died out shortly before this destruction of the dinosaurs, and most of the marsupials also perished; the survivors are found in Australia and South America only. By contrast, the other mammals thrived and spread over the earth's surface.

The major ice ages with alternating warmer interglacial periods have also had their effects on living creatures. At the height of the ice age the sea level is considerably lowered, undergoing a "regression", but with the melting of the ice the sea levels rise, undergoing a "transgression". Not only do the regression and transgression affect the surrounding land but also, by influencing the local temperature, alter the ecosystem, the environment in which the organisms normally flourish most prolifically. This involves the local flora and fauna. It could be said that mass extinctions throw a spanner in the orderly working of the evolutionary process. Certainly the course of evolution depends primarily on external factors; the successful mutant organism is the one that can survive most prolifically in the altered environment. The world is in a state of development no less than the creatures it supports, and we must not be surprised if we suffer illness and death because of the earth's instability. But perhaps we are destined to come to our planet's rescue by living a life of awareness and constant service.

# 3

# *The Creation of Humanity*

The first distinctly human descendant of the ape family was *Homo habilis*, who not only had acquired an upright stature that allowed the hands to be used creatively in the making of tools suitable for hunting but also had a large and complex enough brain to allow reflective thought and language. The transition to *Homo erectus* emphasized these features: it had a larger brain and was able to make simple stone tools. It had more meat in its diet than the other members of the primate order, meat providing a concentrated source of protein and other nutrients far in excess of plants and vegetables. The means of acquiring food were those of hunting and gathering, and the sharing of food brought in its train increasingly complex social interactions. This method of hunting and gathering has been a permanent feature of the biological evolution of the human species from *Homo habilis* and *Homo erectus* to early *Homo sapiens*, and even to some groups of modern humans. The "Bushmen" of the Kalahari Desert (their proper name is !Kung San, the exclamation mark denoting the peculiar clicks and glottal stops of their strange and difficult language) have pursued this way of life up to the present, but are being weaned to the static agricultural way by the local government to suit its own purposes. There is evidence that *Homo erectus* also mastered the use of fire. It is possible that even these primitive humans had a ritual associated with the death of a member of the group.

In due course *Homo erectus* was supplanted by *Homo sapiens*, our own species with its large brain and characteristic cranial features (a forehead that does not slope backwards, unemphatic eye-brow ridges, and an unprotruding flat face with a prominent chin). An early representative was Neanderthal man (*Homo sapiens neanderthalensis*), whose skull retained some primitive features but with a rather larger brain than that of modern man, *Homo sapiens sapiens*, who saw the light of day some 40,000 years ago. Neanderthal man lived between just over 100,000 and 40,000 years ago. His tool-making capacity was quite advanced, and there is clear archaeological evidence of ritual burials which testify to a feeling of awe for the spiritual dimension of life. There was a warm interglacial phase between 130,000 and 70,000 years ago, and then followed the last ice age between 70,000 and 10,000 years ago. Neanderthal man lived during the first part of this ice age; his stocky frame was probably helpful in gaining food during this hard time, but then he was supplanted by our own subspecies *Homo sapiens sapiens*, less hardy but better equipped mentally. When one considers the evolution of man, it would seem that mutations may have taken place in localized populations, and the subsequent dominance was the result of interbreeding as well as natural selection.

*Homo sapiens sapiens* revealed amazing artistic skill soon after his emergence as the dominant human representative. An amazing array of prehistoric, palaeolithic art has been discovered on the walls of various caves in south-west France and north Spain; it has been dated between 35,000 and 10,000 years ago, and its excellence made experts doubt the honesty of the discoverers of the material, who were accused of fraudulently employing modern artists. On the bare walls were painted animals of lifelike vividness: horses, bison and oxen predominated, but other species were also present. With the exception of a few cave paintings in Africa, the human form was sparsely depicted, and birds and fish were also seldom found. In one famous cave in France under the foothills of the Pyrenees two moulded clay bison were found propped up in the middle of a low, round chamber. This sculpture is about 15,000 years old. The significance of all this cave art is debatable, but the consensus of opinion favours the idea of a ritual observance with spiritual overtones. It is certain that the caves, especially their deeper recesses where the most spectacular examples of art are to be found, are painfully inaccessible, especially with the primitive candle illumination available to the people of that time.

Although the human form was seldom depicted in paintings, there are rather rudimentary engravings of people in one site in western France, and statuettes of the female form are also well known. These so-called Venuses have prominent bulbous breasts and buttocks, but there is little attempt at depicting facial features or lower limbs. It may be that a taboo forbade a too-close depiction of the person, whose soul was inviolate. Just as our name is strangely precious, so that we do not divulge it except under social pressure – and the name of God is unmentionable, for then we should be able to control the Deity – so also may have been the physical form of the individual in those far-off days.

It was about 10,000 years ago that the crucial change in life-style occurred among our ancestors: from the previous nomadic hunting and gathering there evolved a more static agricultural existence. Now there was a cultivation of crops, especially cereals, and the taming and domestication of animals rather than their indiscriminate slaughter to assuage the needs of the present moment. In fact, there is some archaeological evidence of the use of animals in the previous period of the later ice age, but nevertheless the transition to a stable agricultural economy was remarkably sudden and universal; only the Australian Aborigines and the North-American Indians persisted with the traditional hunting and gathering up to two centuries ago, and now this way of life is very rare except among the !Kung San whom we have already considered.

The cause of the "agricultural revolution" is uncertain. Amongst possible factors are the warming up of the climate after the ice age, the increase in human population, mental progress in the individuals themselves, and social interdependence. What is certain is the speed at which the human harnessed the local resources for his own ends. Scattered communities grew to form small towns, and the development of trade grew out of the individual talents of respective members. It is reckoned that the first great agricultural surge occurred in the "fertile crescent" area of the Middle East that extends in an arc spanning Israel, Jordan and Syria to the west, Turkey to the north, and Iran to the east. This occurred about 10,000 years ago, and was followed by a similar surge in China about 7,000 years ago and in Mesoamerica (especially Mexico) some 5,000 years ago. At this time there was also advanced maize agriculture in parts of South America, especially Peru, Bolivia and Ecuador. Those people who lived in coastal areas also thrived on the fish of the neighbouring sea.

The essential feature of this period of human evolution was a progressive exploitation of the natural resources. Man no longer merely gathered his daily requirements as he moved on to his next abode; he now made the earth work for him as he domesticated cattle and grew crops. The static mode of life enabled him to think about things other than immediate survival, which his superior intellect had to a large extent guaranteed. He now became an owner, a proprietor, who had to learn the secrets of stewardship, a subject which we thousands of years later are starting to take seriously as the world's resources slowly crumble in the hands of a selfish, predatory humanity. In this respect it is chastening to reflect that acquisitiveness was foreign to the way of life of the groups who hunted and gathered for their existence. What they had obtained was for all to share. After the agricultural revolution the emphasis was on saving, and with it a less openhanded attitude to other people. The static life-style saw the birth of towns, cities, city-states, and finally discrete countries. Concern for one's immediate family circle extended to civic responsibility and national loyalty. The reverse side of this loyalty to one's own fellows has been antagonism to those apart from one.

It is unusual for severe intraspecies assaults to occur in the animal kingdom. Where the means of life of one member are threatened by another there is a display of ferocity sufficient to deter the intruder: the signal, as it were, averts the execution of the message. Even where a fight does occur, the hurt is usually mild. Animals confined and restricted in human custody may show less restrained ferocity when challenged by a fellow member, one of the many sad reflections on the way that man's greed can subvert the natural order of moderation. "Nature, red in tooth and claw", lamented Alfred Tennyson in *In Memoriam*, but in fact the demands made by one animal on another are limited.

The situation is seen also in the hunting and gathering activities of our ancestors before agricultural life came into its own. When the human became a landowner he became increasingly covetous, and the more he acquired, the more he had to defend from the onslaughts of his fellow creatures as well as those of other animals and the natural environment with its storms and droughts.

Friezes and boundary stones found in Peru and Babylon depict armed men and mutilated soldiers. It has been estimated by prehistorians that it was not until the development of the temple towns, about 7,000 years ago, that there is evidence of inflicted death and warfare. It is evident that the human tendency to violence which we all now can appreciate only too well is a cultural acquisition rather than a genetic mutation.

One's mind goes back to the Genesis story once more. When Adam and Eve lived in the primeval paradise God had prepared for them there was no lust, greed or hatred. They had what they wanted but never looked for an excess. But once their personal horizons were extended by the "prince of this world", they were only too aware of their deficiency, seen primarily in a lack of clothing to conceal their genital organs. Their knowledge excluded them from that paradise, and they were sent on their way by God to taste the full rigors of an earthly existence encompassed by toil, pain and mortality. And yet there was hope of a time when the woman's seed would contend with the devil as the evil one contended with that progeny for the mastery of their souls. The battle was to be a spiritual one, for now our allegorical ancestors had truly come of age. In a visionary way the transition of man from a nomadic life of hunting and gathering to one of settled agriculture could be seen as an historic counterpart of the inspired creation story of the Bible and the effects of a disobedience that seems to be an inevitable part of progress to true self-knowledge.

All this is in no way to imply that the primitive hunting and gathering mode of life is preferable to stable agricultural work. Far from it, there seems little doubt that a settled mode of life is a mark of progress inasmuch as it affords time for the individual to contemplate the natural order in tranquil security. The end-result is the creation of a civilization, an advanced stage of social development in which the individual can actualize his full human potential in scientific research, artistic creativity and spiritual aspiration. The Platonic triad of ultimate values that lead us to the spiritual knowledge of God are truth, beauty and goodness (or love in the Christian evaluation). In their pursuit we move beyond the self-seeking ego, losing our very selves in the process, to find our true home in the eternity whose nature is the Deity. And yet the self that is apparently lost is in fact merely eclipsed, so that when we find it once more, it is transfigured into something of the glory of God.

This is the apogee of the creative process, and it is in fellowship with our fellow creatures that its peak is attained, for it is nothing until it is shared unconditionally with all around us. It seems clear that only a fixed society anchored to the earth in confident dependence can aspire to the heights of mortal endeavour. But, as we have already seen, such a society can also descend to the depths of moral degradation in the pursuance of its own material ends to the detriment of all other considerations. Truly the way to heaven has also to traverse hell, ultimately with the purpose of transfiguring it.

The earliest civilizations seem to have arisen in Egypt, Mesopotamia and China. The historical period itself started some 5,000 years ago, and coincided with the Early Bronze Age. It was then that proper writing was fashioned; the Great Pyramids in Egypt were roughly contemporaneous with the Sumerian and Akkadian civilization in Mesopotamia. The Middle Bronze Age, about 3,500 to 4,000 years ago, saw a Sumerian revival in Mesopotamia followed by the first Babylonian dynasty. Abraham arrived in Canaan about 3,850 years ago, and Joseph and his brothers lived in Egypt some 150 years later. The Late Bronze Age, some 3,500 to 3,200 years ago, saw the Exodus of Jews from Egypt towards its close with the ministry of Moses and the proclamation of the Law at Mount Sinai.

The first Iron Age stretched from 3,200 to 2,900 years ago, and was peopled in Palestine by the Judges, Samuel, Saul, David and Solomon. The second Iron Age ended about 2,600 years ago, and saw the dissolution of the alliance between Judah and the northern kingdom of Israel, the tragic moral decline of both kingdoms culminating in the Assyrian deportation of the inhabitants of Israel and the Babylonian deportation of those of Judah over a hundred years later. The return of the Babylonian exiles some seventy years later marked the birth of a mature Judaism that was to be the foundation of Christianity 500 years later and of Islam some 600 years after this.

The beginning of modern civilization as we know it was roughly contemporaneous with the period of Judean exile in Babylon, for at about the same time there was a remarkable efflorescence of spiritual and intellectual enlightenment in Greece, Persia, India, and China. This was to be the foundation of Eurasian supremacy in the world of thought and action. The period around 2,500 years ago had seen the witness of Israel's (using the term in a collective context to include both kingdoms) greatest prophets whose message had been committed to writing, starting with Amos and reaching its peak in the work of Isaiah, Jeremiah and Ezekiel. More or less contemporaneously there was the ministry of Zoroaster in Persia (his birth dates are usually given as 628–551 BC), while in India the Hindu genius blazed forth in the Upanishads, the earliest of which were probably written about 600 BC. The date of the Bhagavad Gita is not known for certain, but it was probably written a few hundred years after the Upanishads. The founder of Jainism, Mahavira, probably died in 468 BC, while Siddhartha, of the family called Gautama, who was to become a supreme Buddha was born in 563 BC and died over eighty years later.

In China there were the complementary spiritual teachers Lao-tzu, who was born in 604 BC and was a principal teacher of Taoism, and K'ung Fu-tse (Confucius) whose dates are 551–479 BC. In Greece the

Athenian civilisation reached its height under Pericles about 470 BC, and its decline was witnessed by Socrates (469–399 BC). His better known pupil Plato (429–347 BC) forms a peak of mystical philosophy, as his equally important pupil Aristotle (384–322 BC) turned away from the mysticism of his master to embark upon a more rationalistic investigation of the world with its human, animal and physical constituents, in the process initiating scientific methodology which was subsequently to guide western, and ultimately world, thought.

This period, from 2,800 to 2,300 years ago, has been called by Karl Jaspers the Axial Era of the world, when humans for the first time simultaneously in Greece, India and China questioned the traditional pattern of life. It was, at least figuratively speaking, a mutation in the human consciousness, though whether there was a corresponding change in the brain's structure as well as function we cannot tell. It is of interest that Jaspers did not include the Hebrew contribution or mention Zoroaster, who influenced the Jewish exiles in Babylon and their successors quite considerably (and through them both Christianity and Islam). Perhaps they are best to be seen as representing the ongoing tradition, quietly but steadily rendered more spiritual, on which Hellenic civilization was to have its most enduring effect as it penetrated the world under the aegis of Jesus and Muhammad.

The story of civilization in America is somewhat different, and deserves a special reflection if only because it is usually barely remembered under the welter of later European ideologies. It seems that the American continent was not inhabited by the human before the *Homo sapiens* stage of development, and man's arrival in the Americas was between 25,000 and 30,000 years ago. The first to arrive were migrant hunters of mongoloid race who entered from Asia by crossing the Bering Straits. These during the ice ages formed a land link with the Aleutian Islands between Siberia and Alaska, from where they moved on through Canada. It is probable that the ice at the foot of the Canadian Rockies blocked this passage for over 10,000 years, and that the main migration occurred between 10,000 and 12,000 years ago. Nevertheless, there is evidence based on radiocarbon dating that the human occupied the Andean area of South America as early as 22,000 years ago, perhaps pioneers of the later, more significant, groups. As we have already noted, the great agricultural surge in America took place some 5,000 years ago, especially in Mexico and the western parts of South America, notably Peru, Bolivia and Ecuador as well as north-west Argentina and the northern part of Chile.

In Mexico the Mayan civilization gradually evolved, later to disintegrate and be replaced by the more advanced Aztecs. The precursors of the Peruvian Incas seem to have been a mixed group of people, but the Chimu seem to have had the greatest impact on the Inca civilization. There was also a Chibcha nation in Colombia, less developed than either the Aztecs or the Incas; there was agriculture, weaving and some trade. The decorative arts in their temples and princely houses as in their ornaments were established elements of their society. Administration was crude, and the religion primitive.

The Aztecs and Incas were decidedly more advanced; a highly centralized, totalitarian administration was noteworthy, and the state of agriculture, architecture, astronomy and also mathematics was surprisingly evolved. The decorative arts were well practised, but neither Aztec nor Inca had developed a system of writing. However, they were able to keep records, the Aztecs with images and some vocal sounds, and the Incas with a skein of different-coloured threads knitted in various ways. There were also some attempts at musical production. Religion was of great importance; it was dark and gruesome, especially with the Aztecs, who practised wholesale human sacrifice. The Incas seem to have been less advanced in their civilization as regards architecture; on the other hand, their religion was less preoccupied with death and was not disfigured by human sacrifice. The absence of a writing skill meant that the "literature" was oral and passed on through the generations. It was only with the Spanish conquests that fragments of recitations were written down. They include prayers, hymns, narrative poems and dramas, love poems and songs. They have a clarity and beauty of expression and feeling. A considerable spiritual "literature" has thus been preserved, and some of it has strongly mystical overtones. There was also a considerable army with fine fighting potential.

What is certain is the inability of either the Aztecs or the Incas to withstand the onslaught of the Spanish invaders, Hernan Cortez conquering Mexico in 1519 and Francisco Pizarro Peru in 1532. The predatory Europeans acted with such callous disregard for the subject people that little was left of the civilizations the conquerors found. The indigenous religions were summarily replaced by an extreme Spanish Catholicism that paid scant respect for the insights of the regional population. However, it has always been the genius of Catholicism to take into its wide compass aspects of local customs (as it did centuries before when it recognized December 25th, the birthday of the Invincible Sun in the Greek mystery-religions, as the day of Jesus's birth).

This eclecticism is especially valuable in our contemporary situation where all the religions are brought close together in a contracting world (due to the ease of travel, the media of mass communication and movements of populations migrating from one part of the world to another). They are all defending their traditional insights against the onslaught of secular ideologies that would reduce spiritual understanding to the level of mere economics or psychology if they had their way. As Jesus would have put it, "He who is not against us is on our side" (Mark 9:40). In this instance a man outside the apostolate was found exorcizing in the name of Christ. It has to be balanced with the contrary dictum, "He who is not with me is against me, and he who does not gather with me scatters" (Matthew 12:30). The matter is one of values, for not everyone who acknowledges Christ in words will enter the kingdom of Heaven, but only those who do the Father's will (Matthew 7:21). Anyone whose heart is set in the right direction is in fellowship with the Son even if he cannot identify him by name. On the other hand, the Church has been at some periods of its history party to terrible cruelty and injustice in the name of Christ; in the end its own power has been forfeited by this treachery.

It is evident, as has already been said, that the indigenous American civilizations were no match for the European one introduced so categorically by the Spanish invaders. Taking the long view, this course of events has proved right: Christianity for all its failings is a higher insight into the nature of God than were the native religions, just as modern science for all its aberrations is a better way to health and understanding the world in which we live than were the ancient philosophies.

And slowly answer'd Arthur from the barge:
The old order changeth, yielding place to new,
and God fulfils himself in many ways,
Lest one good custom should corrupt the world.

This oft-quoted passage from *The Passing of Arthur* sequence of *The Idylls of the King* by Tennyson is indeed wise provided we do not cast the old order derisively aside. It has a habit of reasserting itself if it is not treated with reverence and given its place both in history and in the tenor of our lives. The Christian priest, for instance, when he rehearses the events of the Last Supper in the course of celebrating the Eucharist, should also remember with thanksgiving the exodus of the Israelites from Egyptian slavery that Jesus and his disciples were also recalling on that fateful night.

All the aboriginal inhabitants of the New World are called Amerindians, the latter part of the name commemorating Columbus' misidentification of the Caribbean islands, where he made his first landings, with the Indies of Asia. It is of anthropological interest that the people were indeed of Asian origin, though not of Indian stock. Though the Spanish conquerors behaved with great brutality, it is arguable whether their cruelty was worse than that of the other colonial powers, despite the obloquy frequently levelled against them. At least many of the indigenous people survived – which is more than can be said of some other victims of European imperialism, for instance the Indians of North America – and indeed today form a predominant racial element in a number of Latin American countries, such as Mexico and Peru. They have become the beneficiaries of the Spanish civilization that was to adorn that part of America for three centuries and then be incorporated into the various countries as they attained independence.

# 4

# *Humanity Come of Age*

The last 2,500 years are well known historically because their impact impinges directly on our present situation. The religions of the Far East, being involved with the reality of eternity rather than that of the universe, have had correspondingly less effect on the world situation than have the philosophical systems and spiritualities of the Near East, united as they were to be, to greater or lesser extent, with the Hellenic genius of mystical speculation and scientific exploration. This does not imply an inferior valuation of Indian and Chinese religion, which at the present time is coming increasingly into its own as an essential counter-balance to the arid materialism of the West with its attendent mental and physical disintegration.

The advent of Christianity 2,000 years ago seemed to presage a new stage in human growth: through the sacrifice of God who came down to the world in the form of the Son, taking upon himself the full burden of human weakness after having emptied himself of the divine power that was his by right (in somewhat the same way as God in his eternal mode had effected a shrinkage, or contraction, in order to accommodate the created universe), he was able to bring humanity to a right relationship with the Deity, reconciling the world to God. The creation story of a paradisical state of our original ancestors which was shattered by human disobedience to the divine will does not accord with modern evolutionary theory, but before we cast away the Genesis narrative as mere pre-scientific allegory, we would do wisely to consider its deeper implications. The idea of a prior state of bliss that humans enjoyed and from which they departed is found in Indian and Chinese religion also, and so should be taken seriously rather than viewed with superior condescension. It could mean that the human soul came from a sphere of a different order from the physical body that evolved painfully to its present state of cerebral, and therefore mental, pre-eminence. One remembers with sympathy Wordsworth's beautiful lines from his *Ode: Intimations of Immortality from Recollections of Early Childhood*:

> Our birth is but a sleep and a forgetting:
> The Soul that rises in us, our life's star,
> Hath had elsewhere its setting,
> And cometh from afar,
> Not in entire forgetfulness,
> And not in utter nakedness,
> But trailing clouds of glory do we come
> From God who is our home.

The implication of the soul's pre-existence contained in this passage, while far from scientific proof, rings true to many sensitive people, and the idea need not be summarily dismissed by the arrogance of the marketplace or the dogmatism of the theologian. It is not outside the bounds of possibility that the seat of value judgement which we call the soul should exist in the mental/psychic/spiritual dimension, and find a temporary association with the complex human brain during a person's lifetime, there to gain experience of worldly things in the working-out of relationships with living creatures in general and man in particular. The Freudian psychologist would tend to explain this memory of past bliss, and also the more arresting mystical experiences of union with God that are well documented in the literature of religious studies, to a return to the consciousness of the womb where we felt secure before our expulsion from it at the time of birth. But even if this mechanism were true, the remembrance of greater things in the past could still point to a deeper state of union with God, which could indeed be more easily attainable in the womb (especially if the mother was in peaceful serenity, a not very usual circumstance in worldly life) than after birth into independent existence when the person lay at the mercy of various emotional cross-currents.

It is sad to reflect on the new creation wrought in Christ becoming increasingly tarnished by covetousness for money and power. The new commandment of loving one another was betrayed by the very understandable enmity against the Jews, the children of the old covenant, whose hostility to the new covenant was implacable. This enmity blazed forth in mutual detestation that has only recently been healed. Nevertheless, this fall of Christians from the high, near visionary, path of love for all people, friend and enemy alike, was an inevitable result of the exposing of the full personality, unconscious no less than conscious, of those dedicated to Christ. In him nothing can remain concealed under the deceptive veneer of pious religion. Jesus tells us that if we dwell in the revelation he has brought, we are indeed his disciples: we will know the truth which will set us free (John 8:31–32). This truth is a direct confrontation with our sins, for it is these that enslave us. In communion with Christ we not only see the truth clearly, but we are also able to accept his forgiveness, which frees us from sin's slavery. Only then does the new life commence. But unfortunately it takes a long time for us to come to terms with the destructive elements in our personality, and so healing is correspondingly delayed. Historically the fresh inspiration provided by the new Faith became insidiously encrusted by the urge to worldly power. At the same time the Hellenic springs of Christian theology became increasingly suspect to the hierarchy. The accession of the Church to political power after the agreement with Constantine led to the surfacing of the oppressive aspects of Christianity even if the Roman Empire now became Holy.

Though we are brought to salvation by faith in God alone, we have still to permit the Holy Spirit to initiate a deeper healing of the personality. Then there is a gradual re-creation of the person in the image of God, an image already familiar to the soul in its inner depths. It seems that the human is a bridge uniting the world and God, so that God can work through a willing person to bring order to the material universe. Finally the creation may be filled with the light of the Holy Spirit. Until Christ is a burning presence within us so that he is the inspiration of our life, we remain merely at the foothills of our true vocation, which is to be an agent of light to the world. The preliminary advent of Christ is a mighty light on the path.

With the collapse of the Roman Empire in the fifth century the Dark Ages commenced. Christianity began its slow penetration into northern Europe, but it began to have a decidedly adverse influence further south. It reached a low point in the destruction of the great library of Alexandria, one of the seven wonders of the ancient world. The creative process sprang to the defence of human enlightenment in the unlikely form of the Arab prophet Muhammad, whose dates are believed to be 570 to 632. The teaching of God given to this "seal of the prophets" in the Koran was clear and definitive, but the inquiring human mind will never cease to ask questions, and in due course Greek philosophy found an hospitable home among the more liberal of the Prophet's descendants. It was especially Aristotle that guided their scientific studies, while the great neo-Platonic mystic Plotinus was an important influence on the development of Sufism at about the same time.

While northern Europe languished under a pall of intellectual darkness illuminated by the occasional light of Christian scholastic theology and sanctity, the Muslim world, which then included Spain, enjoyed something of a minor golden age of enlightenment. It was indeed the destructive initiative of the Crusades, aimed at restoring Christian rule to the Holy Land, that brought the semi-pagan soldiery of the Christian West to the knowledge of a distinctly more advanced Islamic civilization. The Christians came to conquer; they left defeated but distinctly more enlightened than at the start of their campaigns, which were attended by barbaric cruelty not only to Muslims and Jews but also to Christians of the Orthodox Church in Constantinople, which was on one occasion sacked by the dissolute army.

The ignorance of the Dark Ages gradually yielded to the enterprise of the Middle Ages, which saw the rise of the great universities and an impressive flourishing of scholastic theology as well as mysticism, the two not infrequently in opposition with one another. The direct experience of God known to the mystic puts human rationality severely in its place, while the reason has to master mystical insight both to interpret its revelation and to check its idiosyncratic excesses. It is here that an authentic religious tradition, by which is meant one that has been proved by the lives and witness of its saints, is of crucial importance, as the great Sufi theologian al-Ghazali showed in relation to Islam. But mystical insight is here also to broaden the way of orthodoxy, which, like everything else in the world, is not static but in a state of continuous creation. Nothing that is fundamentally true need threaten the seeker, for truth, which by its very nature frees us from subservience to idols and brings us closer to the vision of God, draws us to our own fulfilment.

In coming to an assessment of truth, especially in matters spiritual which depend so much on the subtleties of tacit knowledge, there is usually a primary source of enlightenment (usually a scripture), a tradition that has learned to interpret this wisdom over the years, and finally a focus of inner discernment that has two faces. The first is discursive reason based on the scientific findings of the present time, while the second is something much more interior and personal. It is an intuitive awareness of the rightness (or inadequacy) of the matter under consideration, and is a soul quality. It lies beyond mental analysis, but is a mystical appreciation of the validity or otherwise of a teaching. It is mediated directly by the Holy Spirit, but nevertheless requires stern testing by the rational function. In this way intuition and reason may work together, the former pointing the way, the latter then assessing the information to ensure that it is pure, trustworthy and practically sound. In the history of human institutions, especially those associated with religion, these three modalities have often been in conflict. Thus there has been the persecution of mystics in both Christianity and Islam (and on occasion in Judaism also) by a state religion frightened of the threat to an established hierarchy that mystical authority poses. The rationalist has also downgraded mystical illumination because it casts doubt on the absolute inerrancy of reason; "enthusiasm" can be a dangerous word in the ears of the ruling élite – and, of course, it not infrequently goes astray by neglecting the criteria of common sense and rational investigation. It is admittedly true that unchecked mysticism can easily proceed to pantheism, diverting theosophical speculations, and private systems of belief that tail off into frank occultism. Nevertheless, it is the mystic who is generally God's prophet to the world, because he has been privileged to see as much of the divine reality as is compatible with human frailty. His message is nearer the love of God as indicated by Jesus than either that of the theologian or the prelate, unless, of course, representatives of these two disciplines have had a direct mystical encounter themselves. It could, in fact, be insisted that all true theology is mystical inasmuch as a direct encounter with God should precede any thoughts about him.

The Renaissance that followed the Middle Ages witnessed a far less restricted enquiry into the realms of nature. The discovery of new continents opened human awareness to the immensity of the living world, while unobstructed observation established the heliocentricity of our little solar system, in the process provoking a notorious confrontation between clerical dogma and scientific research. Even the full might of the ecclesiastical establishment could not silence the voice of truth, which now, in the mouths of explorers into reality, was the arbiter of a new style of existence. The increasingly uneasy tension between human experience and spiritual tradition culminated in a decisive break in relationship between science and religion during the Age of Reason that dominated the eighteenth century. The spiritual faction tended to use God to explain obscure aspects of the workings of creation, but, very properly, this "god of the gaps", has been ruled out of court by intelligent theologians. As our knowledge increases, so do these gaps become filled in and God is correspondingly eased out of the picture. The furore that followed the publication of Charles Darwin's *On the Origin of Species* some 150 years ago, in which the theory of evolution by natural selection (that we have already considered in a previous chapter) enraged the ecclestiastical powers so that they were made to look ridiculous in a public debate on the subject, saw the end of classical theology as a force governing the world of matter, at least in the eyes of unprejudiced observers. Fundamentalist groups retaliated by stressing the creation narrative of the Bible against all rational evidence, and even today the theory of evolution cannot be taught in some areas that are heavily dominated by the local religious establishment.

On a wider front, the Industrial Revolution of little more than two centuries ago confirmed the supremacy of the scientific approach in the most undeniably practical way. It also demonstrated the superiority of Western culture as its products flooded all countries that could afford to install and use them, so that now countries from all over the world move towards their own sufficiency in industries that at one time would have been the preserve of the West. Our contemporary way of life was heralded by the Industrial Revolution as categorically as was human civilization by the agricultural revolution of 10,000 years ago. When we consider the gradually increasing momentum of human advancement from those prehistoric days to the time immediately preceding the industrialization of society, and compare it with the shattering crescendo of development in our own time, it is evident that the advances over the past century have been far greater than the sum of all earlier material achievements. It is no exaggeration to speak of the technological revolution of the last forty years, for now has power of previously inconceivable magnitude been placed in human hands. We can not only travel in outer space as a preliminary to exploring the other planets of our solar system, but also have the capacity to destroy the entire fabric of the earth.

The break in relationship between science and religion already noted now seems irremediable. The workings of the universe are seen increasingly to be a part of its own nature, not depending on any outside force to supplement them. And yet creation's highest achievement, the human being, has proved himself inadequate to cope with the responsibility of domination that has been thrust upon him (either by

divine decree or the towering mental capacity that
natural selection has given him, according to the
philosophical view of the observer). The mastery of
fire first achieved by *Homo erectus* has found its
apogee not only in the central heating of homes but
also in the incinerators attached to the gas-chambers
of the Nazi concentration camps. Recent developments in the understanding of physics have unle-
ashed the burden of nuclear energy on mankind; it
can be used as a limitless source of power but also
as a way of killing millions of living forms when it
escapes rigorous control, whether in the course of
warfare or during accidents involving nuclear reactors. What does a man gain by winning the whole
world at the cost of his true self? (Mark 8:36).

The situation of mankind was pondered deeply if
not for long by one of the few great prophets of our
century, Dietrich Bonhoeffer, as he lay incarcerated
in prison after the unsuccessful attempt on the life
of Hitler, of which he was an accomplice. His *Letters
and Papers from Prison* edited by Eberhard Bethge
make as compulsive reading now as they did to his
contemporaries forty years ago. He was imprisoned
from April 1943 to the time of his death by hanging
on Monday, April 9th, 1945, a day after he had con-
ducted a little religious service. The concept of the
coming of age of the world was central to his late
thought, for he too realized that God was no longer
necessary to explain the intricacies of the natural process. That type of God was a human artifact and
indeed had to die if man's coming of age was to be

complete. It was the same type of God that the greatest of the Western Christian mystics, Meister Eckhart, had bade us take leave of some six centuries previously.

Among Bonhoeffer's thoughts is the crucial theme, "We should find God in what we do know, not in what we don't; not in outstanding problems, but in those we have already solved", and again, "God cannot be used as a stop-gap. We must not wait until we are at the end of our tether: he must be found at the centre of life: in life and not in death; in health and vigour, and not only in suffering; in activity, and not only in sin. The ground for this lies in the revelation of God in Christ. Christ is the centre of life, and in no sense did he come to answer our unsolved problems." His reflections take him to the conclusion that "God is teaching us that we must live as men who can get along very well without him. The God who is with us is the God who forsakes us (Mark 15:34). The God who makes us live in this world without using him as a working hypothesis is the God before whom we are ever standing. Before God and with him we live without God. God allows himself to be edged out of the world and on to the cross. God is weak and powerless in the world, and that is exactly the way, the only way, in which he can be with us and help us."

However I would add, it is only in the presence of that God that we can start to be mature human beings, not merely ones who, like youngsters in their late teens, have come of age in the eyes of the law and in their physical development.

The uneasy truce between human experience and religious dogma that has attended world history at least since the time of the ancient Greek philosophers was definitively broken with the advent of the Renaissance, and now the rift is very wide. This is especially sad when we remember the impetus given to scientific research by members of various religious orders in the Middle Ages to say nothing of the famous hospitals some of these communities founded. Religion shows itself to its best advantage when it serves the public like Jesus washing the disciples' feet. This is human creation at its finest.

The human has indeed come of age in his power over the natural creation. The sky alone is the limit, but whether he is more fulfilled now than in the long ages past when he hunted and gathered is debatable. Then at least he could share his spoils with his fellows. But the question itself is irrelevant; we are not here simply to be happy. We are to create a new order under the aegis of the God who absents himself for our sake. Is man nature's masterpiece or its Frankenstein's monster? His power to create is seemingly unlimited, but will he bring the earth to full spiritual potentiality or simply submerge it in a sheet of flames?

# 5

# The Springs of Human Creativity

The human is certainly a phenomenon on its own. It shares a bodily configuration with its mammalian relatives and is firmly grounded in mortality, and yet its aspirations reach to the heavens. We have already considered the possibility of an immaterial soul entering a human body with its crowning glory, a brain of enormous intricacy whose subtlety of action far outdistances anything that even its near primate cousins can muster. But even if we take the more usual view of the human mind at birth as having no innate ideas, a so-called *tabula rasa* (erased tablet), it soon acquires a wealth of information that is moulded into opinions both inherited from the person's teachers and imbibed from the local environment. In due course it asserts its power of private judgement. Some of what it learned or took second-hand as truth is found to be inconsistent with its own experience. To be human means to be confronted ceaselessly with a conscience that finds its peace only when it obeys the highest value judgements of authenticity and integrity. Every subterfuge may be taken to avoid or shelve moral responsibility, but until the truth is faced, the person is a living lie unable to confront himself in clear daylight. This inner seat of personal integrity, of moral authority, is called the soul. We remember Jesus' terrible question in the last chapter, "What does a man gain by winning the whole world at the cost of his true self?" This true self is the soul, and it cannot be disregarded for long without a disastrous deterioration in character ensuing. The person reverts to his animal ancestry while retaining the mighty intelligence of the mind ensconced in its impressive palace, the human brain.

The relationship between mind and brain remains a philosophical conundrum. It is certain that there is an intimate connexion between the two during earthly life: severe brain damage can lead to dementia of such an order that a once intelligent person becomes little more than a human vegetable. There is no communication with even closest relatives and dearest friends. It could be that a deeper intelligence remains intact, but such awareness cannot work through the damaged brain and make itself known to the outside world. In the near-death experience that is being reported with increasing frequency, it would appear as if the mind can detach itself from a severely disordered brain, and mediate a consciousness of other worldly brilliance and assurance, but the mechanism of this phenomenon is still under review. It is certain that those who have had such an experience return to mortal life changed people; death ceases to hold any terror for them, while the remainder of their earthly life is invested with a significance of a very different order from the interests and pursuits that had previously attracted them. It may well be that the brain focuses the mind's diverse processes, acting as a channel by which thought touches the world of form in which we are to achieve our aims, pressing on then to fresh endeavours.

Towards the end of the creation story we read, "So God created man in his own image; in the image of God he created him; male and female he created them" (Genesis 1:27). What then is this image of God in which humanity is moulded? Since no one has ever seen God, and indeed his presence is surrounded by a radiance that blinds mortal sight by its sheer intensity, there can be no physical likeness of God in our world. "What likeness will you find for God or what form to resemble his?" asks Isaiah (40:18). In 42:8 we read, "I am the Lord; the Lord is my name; I will not give my glory to another god, nor my praise to any idol." And yet God has imparted some of his glory to humanity, fully manifest, at least in Christian eyes, in the person of the Lord Jesus. This glory is an intuitive appreciation of the divine presence which serves not merely to know God but also to transfigure the person. We know God most perfectly when we resemble him most closely in our attitude to the world and the service that pours out in burning love for all that exists. It is thus that we may fathom the statement that we are created in the divine image. The function of the soul that knows God in deep relationship is called the spirit; according to its development the soul can receive the Spirit of God, the Holy Spirit, by virtue of its own spirit, which can, using a spatial metaphor, be defined as the deepest, yet most exalted, point of the soul. Alternatively it may be that the Holy Spirit lies immanent in the human soul in its spirit, but that he has to be born as a conscious presence before the person can know God and do the work of love that lies before him.

It is this work that God has destined for us, and we will never know complete rest until we have actualized our identity as creatures formed in the divine image by carrying out that work. The action of the soul is the will, and its freedom will determine how and when we perform the task set before us. God himself is powerless to command us by virtue of his prior gift of free will. And so we are in very fact gods in our own right, as Psalm 82:6 asserts. But the sentence proceeds with the warning that we shall die as frail humans, even as princes fall, so long as our attitude to our neighbours is unsatisfactory. A god in this context is a being with independent will, an autonomous creature. But it is a lamentable fact that until the individual will is aligned to the divine purpose that looks for the healing of all that is disturbed and awry, whatever is attempted by the creature will go wrong.

God creates out of unbounded love, and while he gives his creatures free rein to work out their own pattern of life, he is never far from them in his overflowing love: "As a father has compassion on his children, so has the Lord compassion on all who fear him" (Psalm 103:13). This fear is not that of a slave to his master, but a sense of awe at the marvel of life and the privilege we all share in inhabiting the world. St Paul in Romans 8:14–15 puts it thus: "For all who are moved by the Spirit of God are sons of God. The Spirit you have received is not a spirit of slavery leading you back into a life of fear, but a Spirit that makes us sons, enabling us to cry 'Abba! Father!' " When we recall Jesus' exclamation of these same words at the peak of his trial at Gethsemane, we can see the height of the destiny set for us who are his co-heirs. For this is the end of human creation, and its price is severe in the suffering it entails.

The free will of the rational creature shows itself in his capacity to alter the environment according to his own choice. This ability to change the existing order is the essence of creativity. In this respect we should remember that the universe itself is in a state of constant creation. The "big bang" of 15,000 million years ago began the process of creation, but the universe has not stood still from then. Its inherent instability is the source of intramundane calamities like earthquakes and hurricanes, but the fecundity of living forms even in our small planet stresses its creative potential also. Jesus said, "My Father has never yet ceased his work, and I am working too" (John 5:17). This statement infuriated his audience because, by calling God his own Father, he was claiming equality with God. And yet the purpose and also the privilege of the human is to do exactly what Jesus claimed, to assist the Creator in the world's maintenance and its expansion into new creative channels. However, only when the human attains something of a Christ-like stature will he be able to play his part with mature responsibility. Until then he is more likely to act irresponsibly and put the creation in jeopardy.

An act of creativity shared by all living organisms is the process of giving birth. So fundamental an event is it that the will can scarcely be included in its action, at least in respect of the less rationally endowed humbler forms of life. It is only the mammals that accommodate their fertilized ovum within themselves, carrying the embryo until it is sufficiently viable to be born into an indifferent world. The woman especially can exult in the gestation of a new individual within her own body until the time of painful, yet glorious, release at its birth into independent existence. Thus is a woman fulfilled of her special creative function, the profundity of which the attendant man can never fathom. He, by contrast, lives more easily in the world of the mind and spirit as he schemes to change the material universe.

We recall with sympathy Eve's exultant cry when she had lain with Adam and given birth to Cain, "With the help of the Lord I have brought a man into being" (Genesis 4:1); the accompanying pains of labour decreed by God as a punishment for the disobedient woman (Genesis 3:16) pale into insignificance when the fruit of procreation is tasted, one that is later to kill his gentle, inoffensive brother Abel. Jesus, in John 16:21, compares the passing anguish of the parturient woman with the immediate state of sorrow that will follow his crucifixion, soon to be followed by the triumphant resurrection. Here there will be no repudiation of past associations, only a restoration of friendship with an intimacy of a warmer radiance than the disciples had known during their earthly work with their Master.

The act of procreation is the prototype of all other human creative ventures. Its impetus lies outside the compass of the person's will, for it is a pure gift of God (or the natural order, for the intransigent agnostic). Nevertheless, the full cooperation of the individual is essential if the divine grace is to make its impact on the person's awareness. Only then is a creative process initiated, and the strain brought about by the sheer labour and emotional tension accompanying the work, whether of art or science, is comparable in its own proportions to the pain of a woman giving birth to her child. When we think about the cavalier way in which humans treat procreation, we can only wonder at the generosity of the Creator and the careless abandon of his creatures.

Creativity is indeed at the very heart of human existence. The human, like his Creator, is unceasingly involved, while his health is intact, in pursuing fresh lines of thought and starting new ventures that give him more effective control over his environment. It is the intellectual faculty of imagination that sets the creative impulse on fire, but the imagination itself is informed by an inspiration that impinges on the mind from a source beyond its compass. That source cannot be provoked into action, being in fact the Holy Spirit which, like the wind, blows where it will and is not subject to human manipulation. Indeed, the more it is invoked, the more likely it is to withdraw, as it were drying up. No fresh input will enter the mind until the person becomes fully receptive. This entails a condition of absolute humility in which the ego lies low in obedient service and not its customary selfish domination. This state of humility involves a full dedication of the person to the ultimate values of truth, beauty and love; which of these takes precedence depends on the nature of the creative work, whether scientific, artistic or philanthropic. But in the end all three are one inasmuch as each leads to the original source and ultimate end, whose name is God.

Once the imagination is activated, the will is mobilized into putting the inspiration from mere thought into action. At first, the idea that appeals to the person has a selfish quality and is concerned with what appears to be the individual's immediate benefit and that of those closest to him in blood ties or emotional sympathy. At this stage the human is like a growing child, entranced by the power so lavishly bestowed upon him: he can create and destroy as visions of dominating his little world flood into his alert, receptive mind. Experience teaches him that without love of other people, private schemes fail in their purpose.

Thought is certainly the antecedent and stimulus of effective action. Its creative potential is immense, but it is usually dissipated in ever-diminishing circles of ineffectual speculation. This is a consequence of our usual state of inattention to the present moment as our minds roam disconsolately over the past which cannot be changed, while the menace of the future often directs us into imaginary confrontations with adversaries and circumstances that exist primarily, if not entirely, in our own minds. Well does Jesus remind us that however much we may worry about things, we cannot alter the course of nature thereby; anxious thought cannot add an inch to our height. The tendency to meet troubles half way, by imagining what might happen if a certain course of events were to ensue, actually stifles the higher imaginative faculty, because the dark cloud of anguish blocks the entry of the inspiration of the Holy Spirit. Pascal remarked that the human is merely a reed, the weakest thing in nature, but he is a thinking reed. He might well have gone on to observe that thought is both the midwife of the new dispensation and the spouse of suicide. We do not think properly when we are in turmoil within. By contrast, fruitful thought occurs when we are completely aware of the present moment. Then the mind is fully conscious of the void, the very emptiness of God in which creation finds its place of operation. This is, in fact, the state of pure contemplation: the mind is alert and actively receptive, waiting in undivided attention for the divine presence to inform it. This it does by showing it a higher purpose and revealing a deeper meaning to the present events. This divine presence is the Holy Spirit himself, but he can make himself known only when the person is quiet and of untroubled mind. Then the door of the soul is open so that the Spirit of God can enter unimpeded.

Of course, it could be argued that this rather awesome process of creative imagining belongs to the realm of genius and sanctity rather than the world of everyday activity. While the peaks of contemplative inspiration are indeed attained by exceptional individuals, the less exalted moments of creative illumination that come to us all when we are living in an ordinary way also tend to be preceded by a silence born of acknowledged ignorance. When the mind is at the end of its tether and can find no other place of help, God may be able to make his presence felt, and then a solution may suddenly lighten up the seemingly impenetrable darkness. This does not mean that the Deity suddenly appears to provide a magical answer to our problems; he sets in motion a harmonious collaboration between inspiration and thought, between emotion and reason, and then a previously insoluble problem is easily confronted and clarified.

A fine example of this principle is the silence that Job and his companions attain in the face of the enigma of undeserved suffering that finds no rational answer. At this point God shows himself directly to Job. The revelation impresses on Job the impotence of human reason, in respect of divine purpose, and a new understanding of reality dawns on him: the creative process is so vast that the aches and pains of any one creature are an inevitable part of the working-out of God's love that will not interfere with the freedom of action he has given all living forms, and especially the human with his uniquely powerful mind. Nevertheless, God waits patiently for the creature to fulfil its own destiny of perfection, and he will never fail to respond with help once this is requested. As we have already noted, divine assistance strengthens the faculties of the mind, so that we, in cooperation with the Creator, can solve our personal problems and serve the whole creation in selfless devotion. A real love helps the beloved grow into maturity through a progressive mastery of the impinging challenge. If the challenge were simply to be removed, the beloved would remain as weak and ineffectual as before. The secret of creativity is contained in this confrontation and our gradual victory over it.

It therefore comes about that human creativity has two components. First, there is receptivity to a power beyond our rational grasp, one that pours down the inspiration of God into our clear consciousness, and second, a lucid thinking process whereby the inspiration is brought down to earth so as to become the source of a plan of action. This action may be a simple planning of a day's activity or a projected holiday excursion, or it may be a complex philosophical investigation or a detailed research scheme. How the person uses what has been given from on high depends on his own state of spiritual awareness. We remember Jesus' remark that God makes his sun rise on good and bad alike, and sends his rain on the honest and dishonest (Matthew 5:45). The good and the honest will use these divine gifts profitably, whereas the evil-doer will either squander them or else use their produce for destructive purposes. It cannot be denied that some human skill has had a destructive effect on the environment, as much through ignorance as malice.

Human creativity depends also on such secondary factors as diligence of study, perseverance and humility. This last can be defined as a state of inner silence in which the person can learn from the circumstances around him, especially the failures that mar his path and the little people who are generally disregarded, but whose native wisdom may contain an element of truth denied even the experts in the field. Jesus undoubtedly taught wisdom to all who had the foresight to hear him, but we may be sure he also learned much about human nature from the many people he met in his daily ministry. All effective dialogue has a creative potential, and frank, open relationships, such as Jesus initiated in his mixing with all strata of the local society especially at their humble festivities, are of great importance in widening the creative potential of any inspired individual.

In the fascinating story of the Tower of Babel we see the end of human creativity in a selfish context. God is eclipsed by the urgency of human desire; though the provider of all things, he, as in the story of Adam and Eve, is unceremoniously ignored in the human thrust for ultimate power. We need not take God's concern lest he be outshone by his creatures too seriously; a more realistic exegesis is the inevitable discord that results from people taking the sacred gift of inspiration into their own hands without reference to their Creator. Human institutions will always fail as personalities clash; only the divine love can make the institution secure. This indeed is the meaning of the Church, and it has miraculously stayed firm despite the constant attack of the powers of death (Matthew 16:18). These powers, the same in essence as those that led the builders of the Tower of Babel, are demonic in origin, but use covetous humans for their execution. The Christian Church, unlike its secular counterpart, though frequently rocked by dissension and torn apart by schism, has never lost its common language, so powerful is the love of Christ among his dissident flock. By contrast, the secular city, typified by the Tower of Babel, dissolves into internecine strife as the human will becomes dominant and each person seeks his own satisfaction without reference to the others. The common language is lost as love departs and each member retreats into his own fastness. The end, ironically, is disintegrative war and not the splendid Tower of Babel set to eclipse the small creations of God.

When we consider the amazingly emergent creativity of the human in our own century, the force of its destructive potential seems far to have outweighed any constructive endeavour, which, indeed, has often been incinerated in the furnaces of hatred that lie just below the juvenile mind set on conquering the world. But even in this darkness a greater light is gradually dawning, as the human is learning about the responsibility to the natural order that underlies the privilege of his enormous mental capacity. It is evident that there are different grades of creativity, from the artful deception of the criminal to the well-pondered schemes of the philanthropist, from the destructive genius of the Nazis in their erection of the vile gas chambers to the painful, selfless dedication of the medical research worker engaged in his constant encounter with disease and his endeavours to overcome those afflictions that remain incurable at the present time. A composer creates a new piece of music, which may then be created anew by an inspired interpreter acting either as soloist or orchestral conductor. The declaration in Revelation 21:5 is eternally valid, "Behold. I am making all things new." This is the emergent creation of the universe that will find its summation when everything is lifted up to its creator, resurrected from the thraldom of matter to the liberty of pure spirit, as the body of Christ changed from the inertia of dead matter to the vibrancy of transformed spirit.

The human has indeed been made in the image of God. By his brilliant intellect he can trace the ways of the process of evolution, entering into the sheer grandeur of the mind of the Creator, who both fashions creatures out of nothing and allows them to proceed with their own lives in complete freedom. By his spirit the human is privileged to enter into a relationship of great intimacy with the Creator so that he can come to resemble him as closely as befits a mere creature at the heavenly table. The essence of the human dilemma is the alignment of mind and spirit, of body and soul. Until creation is a truly spiritual event it is destined to crumble into chaos, but once it is spiritually directed, it has the power to change the whole universe into something of the nature of God, seen as Jesus Christ in Christian terms. No other creature, at least within our world, has this power, hence the special place prepared for the human in the pageant of life. Jesus reminds us that, cheap as they are, sparrows may not fall to the ground without our Father's leave (since they too are under the law of life and death, of purposive action and gravity). And even the hairs of our head have all been counted, for there are a finite, though vast, number of hair follicles in the scalp, as amazing a fact in its compact brevity as the magnitude of the universe is in its complexity. Above all, we need have no fear, for we are worth more than any number of sparrows (Matthew 10:29–31).

# 6

# *Man and Nature*

There is no doubt that the human by virtue of his superior intellect is in charge of the natural order. Even the fiercest beasts that could destroy a man in a trice in physical combat have learned by bitter experience to slink away at the approach of the human. Not a few species have disappeared from the earth's face since the advent of human rule, and now the situation is so desperate that the earth could well be totally depopulated of all its natural fauna. Only those animals that the human has learned to domesticate for his own use or pleasure would stand any chance of survival were it not for wiser counsels that are realizing that man and nature are in delicate symbiosis and that the human cannot survive in a world depopulated of its natural flora and fauna. A useful account of the endangering of species and the preservation of a few of them by international agencies is contained in the fine book *Back from the Brink*, subtitled *Success in Wildlife Preservation*, written by Guy Mountford, a noted figure in this field. It was published in 1978, but its message is as relevant today as then, and the examples considered here are taken from his account of the matter.

A rare species of antelope, the Arabian oryx, a beautiful desert creature, has from time immemorial been slain by the Beduin as a source of food, but the real threat to the animal's survival followed the arrival of commercialized hunting parties from many countries. Largely through the concern of a single person, Ian Grimwood, who saw the danger in time, the remaining few oryxes were saved and rehoused elsewhere. The breeding stock thus cultivated have now been sent back to Arabia and the neighbouring countries where natural reserves have been set up by the governments concerned aided by the World Wildlife Fund and the Survival Service Commission of the International Union for the Conservation of Nature. It required the solicitude of a foreigner to alert the countries themselves to the peril of wildlife extinction.

The havoc wrought by big-game hunters has been seen in the terrible slaughter of leopards and tigers in India. The near extermination of these species has been facilitated by the wholesale destruction of the tropical forests carried out by commercial interests. Both the tree wood and the land, which is available for building factories and other installations, are valuable to them. The deer living in these moist deciduous forests are destroyed, so that a source of food for these fierce carnivores is removed; in addition, some species of deer are themselves destroyed in this irresponsible exploitation of the forests. As we have already noted, "nature red in tooth and claw" may

be vicious, but at least it knows its level of satiety.
The human, by contrast, is obsessed with gluttony.

> Tyger, Tyger, burning bright
> In the forests of the night,
> What immortal hand or eye,
> Dare frame thy fearful symmetry?

So wrote William Blake in his *Songs of Experience*. He
was meditating on God's mysterious ways in fashioning such a destructive beast. Today this terror of the
jungle has been largely wiped out by a greater terror,
the human being. Guy Mountford, himself a tiger
lover, was appalled to find out that the 100,000 Asian
tigers of the 1920s had been reduced in number to
barely 5,000 in 1967. In addition to starvation and
big-game hunting there was also a flourishing trade
in tiger-skin coats and rugs. The fur trade was stimu-
lating the shooting, trapping and poisoning of existing tigers. Of course, tigers can kill village cattle and
also humans, but this happens usually only when
their basic prey, old and sickly deer and wild pigs,
are scarce, as, for instance, when hunters have shot
all the deer and pigs near villages. In fact, in natural
conditions the tiger has an important ecological role
in disposing of old and sickly deer and wild pigs in
Asia, thus maintaining the virility of their own wild
population. Man-eating tigers are usually found to
have been prevented from hunting their usual prey
on account of injury or old age.

In the preservation of such a creature as a tiger,
zoos cannot cater for their life of swimming and hunt-

ing. Mountford makes the point that neither zoos nor "safari parks" help in wildlife preservation since they are motivated by exhibiting animals for human entertainment, though admittedly they may have an educational value. A tiger in captivity becomes lethargic and develops progressive cerebral degeneration; a tigress in captivity tends to neglect or eat her cubs, whereas in the wild she would teach them to hunt. This cannot be done in captivity. In fact, if such offspring were to be returned to the wild, they would be incapable of hunting wild prey. They would either starve, or else be killed by other tigers. Alternatively, they would be obliged to take to easy prey such as village cattle or villagers themselves.

Through the agitation of Mountford there are now tiger reserves in India, Nepal, Bangladesh and Bhutan: thus the Indian race of tigers has been protected. Similar action is being taken by Indonesia to save the Sumatran and Javan races, while Malaysia and Thailand have reserves for the Indo-Chinese race. The USSR has improved the guarding of its Siberian tigers, and even China, formerly quite aloof, has put its remaining tigers under protection. Furthermore, nearly all the countries of Asia have banned tiger hunting and the export of skins, such as were previously used for women's coats. This rather detailed discussion about a single endangered species indicates not only the main sources of danger but also practical ways of dealing with the problem.

Another mammal severely endangered is the rhinoceros, the second largest surviving land mammal (the elephant, also endangered, is the largest). Its massive hide is its protection, but its weight, short legs and poor sight render it very vulnerable to predators. Nevertheless, it survived quite well until the belief arose in China and neighbouring countries that the ground-up horn of a rhinoceros was a powerful aphrodisiac. This belief and the high prices paid for the horns were driving the species to extinction. In fact, every part of the animal has commercial value: hide, hair, blood, nails, internal organs, urine, and the horns (which are composed of compacted hair). The urine is reputed to be an asthma cure, while the magical properties of the animal are still widely credited; cups carved from the horn are supposed to disintegrate if a jealous spouse is trying to administer poison in the drink. All this shows that primitive superstition can be as effective a way of exterminating a species as modern industrial development. At any rate, the rhinoceros is now protected in national parks and reserves in Uganda and Indonesia. The African rhinoceros is killed by certain tribes who are brave enough to spear it as a proof of their manhood, but the real slaughter is by wire foot-snares which are tethered to a heavy log which the animal drags through the bush until it is exhausted; elephants are also killed in this way, since the ivory of their tusks, like rhinoceros horn, are shipped to the Far East. It is poachers who carry out this gruesome trade.

The Murchison Falls National Park, now called the Kabalega Falls National Park, in Uganda, where the Albert Nile confluences with the Victoria Nile, is a sanctuary where rhinoceros and elephant continue to thrive together with the largest surviving population of crocodiles to be found anywhere in Africa. The Republic of South Africa has also played its part in ensuring the survival of the species. In the Umfolozi Game Reserve in Natal the remnant of the white rhinoceros were guarded, and when the numbers increased, some were transported to areas in southern and central Africa where they formerly existed. But they were sent only where properly protected reserves or national parks were available to receive them.

An example of a species that was nearly exterminated in the Andean area is the vicuña, a tawny-coloured, rather gazelle-like animal with tufts of fleecy white hair dropping from its long neck. Its wool was used for making clothes by the Spanish and Portuguese invaders, who, unlike their Inca predecessors, had no concern for the preservation of the environment. Once more, the crusade of a single dedicated person, Felipe Benavidas, has resulted in the development of national parks and reserves in Chile, Peru, Bolivia and Argentina, where a considerable number of these endangered animals now procreate. Other animals whose skins have been used for human adornment are the fur seals, jaguars and ocelots, but vicuña garments have tended to be a special attraction.

An animal much closer to the human is his ape cousin, the orang-utan, a Malay name meaning "man of the jungle". From its natural habitat in Malaysia and Indonesia it has, for a long time, been captured and transported to Europe and America; the mothers are often shot and the babes secured alive, for the breeding record of these animals in captivity is poor: they become fat and lethargic, and die prematurely. The problem here was to save the orphaned young, rehabilitate them, and then return them to their natural environment. Two names are predominant in this venture, Barbara Harrisson, who specialized in rescuing and rearing baby orang-utans, and John McKinnon, who studied these apes by quite literally living among them for months at a time in their native rainforest. Mrs Harrisson found that the growing animals were extremely destructive to her garden and that it was important to send them back to their wonted forest habitation. Rehabilitation centres were set up using the information that John McKinnon had acquired about the natural disposition of the orang-utan before the animals were returned to the wild By nature they are solitary, moving alone or in small family groups from one fruiting tree to another and occupying a tree-top nest for so long as it takes to strip the tree of fruit. Unfortunately the destruction of the Indonesian rain-forests threatens the survival of the species.

A good example of thoughtless human interference with the local ecology having baneful general consequences is the fate of the giant pied-billed grebe (a short-bodied, lobe-footed, almost tailless diving bird) on Lake Atitlán in Guatemala. Large-mouthed bass were introduced into the lake to improve sport-fish-ing. The consequences were disastrous, for the fish preyed on the young water-birds, including nestling giant grebes. Furthermore, the freshwater crabs were driven to deeper waters with a resulting loss of food for the Indians, who as a consequence took to more waterfowl, including grebes. The reed cutting they carried out in pursuit of their quarry diminished the breeding habitat for the grebes. Once more it was the initiative of a single person, Anne La Bastille, that checked the havoc. The whole episode stresses a fundamental principle: the thoughtless introduction of alien species of animals or plants almost invariably results in a chain-reaction of disasters such as these.

There are still in our crowded world isolated oases of tranquillity where the native fauna and flora have been left relatively undisturbed by human invaders. The most celebrated example is the Galapagos Islands under the protection of Ecuador that we have already mentioned with reference to Charles Darwin and his seminal work on the evolution of species. Galápago is Spanish for tortoise, and it was the prospect of obtaining the remarkable giant tortoises native to the islands that first attracted ships to these inhospitable regions. Darwin noted how these creatures ambled slowly on without the least sign of fear of the surrounding sailors. It is estimated that the wildlife of these islands has been evolving for at least a million years, hitherto in almost complete isolation. This isolation from the stabilizing influence of a constant genetic interchange, such as occurs in a continental landmass, has encouraged the creation of new species. The bird and reptile colonists were free to experiment and occupy ecological niches which, on the mainland, were chosen by other species. In the absence of competitors those which succeeded in adapting to the new environment were free to evolve new feeding behaviour and to develop in a direction most suited to their new existence.

The unwelcome visitation of the human has brought its tale of woe: not only do tourists have an adverse psychological effect on animal behaviour, but there has also been the introduction of animals foreign to the part that have ravaged the native species. Amongst these pests are dogs, cats, goats and rats as well as pigs, donkeys and cattle. In this connexion, goats, dogs and rats in a wild state are virtually impossible to eradicate. These, and the Wasmannia fire-ant, are scourges to the island ecosystem.

It is especially moving to read how the birds and other native animals treat the human visitor so trustingly, as though he was a passing friend. It brings one back to the prophecy of Isaiah 11:6–9, where all the animals live in harmony, led by a little child. Certainly the earth knew far greater peace before the human made his tempestuous appearance, but no doubt a higher peace will follow mankind's civilization to a maturity that surpasses the mere coming of age of an impetuous youngster. At present the policy of conservation rigorously pursued by Ecuador has been helped by the Charles Darwin Foundation for the Galapagos set up in 1959. There is also the

Charles Darwin Research Station established on one of the islands for the preservation of the tortoises.

When one considers the effect of foreign animals on the native fauna, one is also reminded of the scourge of European disease bequeathed to the natives of America and Polynesia; smallpox and measles undoubtedly caused more deaths than the brutality of the foreign invaders. On the other hand, the native Indians of America may have transmitted syphilis to the sailors commanded by Columbus during his stay in the New World (the situation is complicated by the fact that a number of non-venereal diseases are caused by organisms indistinguishable from the one associated with syphilis, and it might be that one of these underwent a mutation to that causing the venereal disease).

Mountford, in the final assessment of the task ahead which concludes his excellent survey, sees the fundamental threat to all wildlife, and indeed to all life, on earth as a combination of the population explosion and the unbridled excesses of modern technology which can now destroy rain-forests on a massive scale. What is happening to wildlife and the habitats of all wild creatures is, as he says, the writing on the wall for our own survival. While hungry nomadic people, such as those living in the highlands of central Asia, must shoot or trap animals to keep alive and clothe themselves against the bitter winter climate, those living in the jungles of the tropics can live more easily in equilibrium with nature, destroying little except for their immediate frugal needs, since neither food nor clothes is a problem. In such regions conservation difficulties are almost entirely concerned with unwise government land-use policies. In order to obtain quick cash returns in foreign currencies, mineral and forest rights are leased to foreign companies. The exploitation of marine resources, such as the harvesting of whales, fur seals, turtles and fish, especially in South American waters, is also largely in foreign hands. The inequitable use of declining natural resources for the benefit of the rich nations can only make the acceptance of wise conservation measures by the developing countries more difficult to obtain. Unfortunately the funds available are small in comparison with the magnitude of the problem. However, since prevention is better than cure, education of the general public is essential, and a conservative strategy should be applied for areas containing representative samples or exceptional communities of plants or animals.

In fact, the general public has of late been alerted to the pollution of the environment by disastrous industrial wastes, a matter not considered by Mountford. The terrible "smogs" that used to clog the atmosphere of Britain earlier in the century have been ended by the Smoke Abatement Act; numerous elderly people now survive the winters who would previously have succumbed to acute chest infections. The hazard of nuclear fallout, first brought to the attention of a barely credulous world in 1945 when atom bombs rained down on the intransigent Japanese at the end of the Second World War, has

been highlighted more recently by disasters involving nuclear reactors; what the ultimate cancer risk for
the world's population as a whole will be we all
wait anxiously to know. But the more commonplace
industrial wastes belched into the atmosphere are not
without their problems. One is "acid rain" which
follows the solution of sulphur dioxide and nitrogen
peroxide in the atmospheric water that subsequently
falls as rain on the parched earth. That falling on
lakes may contribute an acidity sufficient to kill the
fish in them.

Another current problem is the "greenhouse
effect" due to waste gas, mostly carbon dioxide, in
the atmosphere trapping more and more of the sun's
heat. Gases released into the atmosphere as a result
of human industrial and agricultural activities are
called anthropogenic gases, and their effects can be
of great detriment to the world's atmosphere. In
respect of the greenhouse effect, not only will there
be a general rise in global temperature, but there will
also follow severe shortages of water in many parts of
the world, especially the Middle East and California.
Hurricanes will also be more frequent.

A third hazard of anthropogenic gases is the effect
of chlorofluorocarbons on the ozone layer of the
atmosphere; this protects the earth from excessive
exposure to ultraviolet light which causes skin cancer
in those of fair complexion. Indeed, the predomi-
nance of dark-skinned people in the tropical areas is
a good example of natural selection, for the melanin
pigment in their skin protects it against the baneful

effects of ultraviolet light. On the other hand, the black groups are at a disadvantage in cold climates, for ultraviolet light also activates a fatty substance in the skin to produce vitamin D, which is essential for the normal growth and maintenance of bones. Without it the bones soften, and in the young rickets may also occur. Therefore the fair-skinned groups thrive in the temperate and polar areas of the globe. Fortunately adequate doses of the vitamin are present in various animal products, provided, of course, the person can afford to buy them.

It is interesting that the wholesale burning of tropical rain-forests is an important contributory factor to the greenhouse effect, indicating how the predatory human may start by destroying natural flora and fauna, only in the end to endanger his own existence also. On the other hand, these forests yield essential wood and fuel resources for the local population. Likewise, the factories that belch forth their share of anthropogenic gases, including the aerosols of chlorofluorocarbons, give employment to thousands while providing essential energy for other work necessary in a civilized society. It may well, ironically, come to pass that nuclear power, which arouses such strong emotional opposition amongst conservationist groups, is potentially the safest source of energy production. Certainly both coal and oil produce pollution on a scale far greater than that associated with the smoke-filled fog of previous times.

It is not surprising that the theme of conservation

is on the lips of all aware people. A line has somehow and somewhere to be drawn between the essential needs of populations faced with starvation if they do not kill the local fauna, and the greed of nations concerned with little more than the impersonal control that is the basis of power. The "Green" political parties are still not governing any particular country, but their voice has to be heard by the major parties both in power and in opposition. It is unfortunate that some conservationists are fanatical to the extent of attempting to destroy nuclear and other dangerous installations, because their very hatred produces a counter reaction among the more staid members of society, a situation seen also among "animal rights" groups whose hatred of biological experimentalists seems sometimes to be greater than their concern for the animals used in the medical research. Nevertheless, the motivation behind the activities of conservationists and those opposed to the use of animals for medical research is well grounded; without these dedicated, if irritating, people both the environment and sentient animals would be much more subject to exploitation and mutilation by obtuse, power-directed humans. When a scientific research worker is in control, he can all too easily forget the feelings of the animals he is using for his studies. He believes that the control and removal of human suffering is his goal, while in fact fame is often the spur. Yet the value of inspired experimentation has been beyond measure in understanding normal animal physiology as a preliminary to dealing with both animal and human disease. We have to live in an evolving world, choosing frequently between the lesser of two unpleasant situations, in this instance human and animal disease versus the use of animals (and sometimes humans too, provided they have given prior consent) as research tools with the inevitable suffering this may cause even after all efforts have been made to reduce pain to a minimum. When a person is in agony, his strongest convictions soon evaporate under the scorching need for immediate relief.

Do animals have souls? If the word is used in the context of a centre of unique identity, I believe the answer must lie in the affirmative. Any sentient creature, one having the power of sense-perception, has the rudiment of a soul, and the more developed the intelligence of that creature, the more emphatic is its individuality. It feels terror when threatened, and dreads extinction. But the human soul is something more than this: it embraces an appreciation of higher values (truth, beauty and love) and is in conscious contact with a transcendent source which we call God (or the eternal ground of being for those of non-theistic belief like the Buddhist – in this context the difference does not matter very much). Whether this soul is brought in at the time of conception, as we have already considered, or whether it is "made" (as Keats put it) in the course of incarnate life, as would be the usual view of the matter, it seems to have shown itself categorically at the time of the evolution of the earliest of the human sub-species, *Homo habilis*, who not only fashioned tools creatively but also had

ipressively developed brain structure sufficient
language and reflective thought. His successor,
*Homo erectus*, seems to have had an awareness of the
Numinous, if the suggestions of a ritual associated
with the death of a member of the group are valid.
The human soul points beyond itself, and this is the
source of religion, an attitude of mind that stubbornly
resists all the attempts of the rationalist to dislodge
(indeed, the negative enthusiasm of the rationalist is
itself a response to the numinous dimension, which
his pride will not allow him to acknowledge, since,
like Adam and Eve, he wants undisputed power over
the whole world, an approach strengthened by the
human perversions so often fostered by immature
religious traditions). The debate between the rationalist and the believer is essential for the growth of
the soul; the impact of evolutionary theory on
religious belief is a fine example of this painful, but
essential, trend, this vital synthesis of reason and
belief.

It seems probable that closely domesticated animals, especially beloved pets, acquire something of
the soul quality of their owners. The work of guide
dogs shepherding the blind is an especially moving
testimonial of the responsible care an animal can
have for a human. It is probable that animals have
powers of extrasensory perception, though admittedly some of the tales told are embellished by the
enthusiasm of people with psychic interests. At any
rate, this all emphasizes the important role the
human has to play in both the preservation and

elevation of his animal brethren. The record has so far been chequered, but a better dispensation may be on the way.

Should we eat animal flesh? It would indeed be good if we could return to the state of our allegorical ancestors Adam and Eve, who, like the animals, fed exclusively on plants, but this is not possible for everybody. It seems that the evolving human added meat to his diet as a ready source of protein for his existence of hunting and gathering, thereby diverging from his vegetarian ape cousins. Today there are, apart from those religious groups (notably Hindu and Buddhist) who eschew meat, many people of the West who are moving towards a plant diet. Provided this is done with a careful concern for nutritional values, this is all to the good, but cranky diets can cause much harm. A vegetarian dietary regime should not be undertaken lightly, nor should the concept of vegetarianism fill its practitioners with an attitude of spiritual superiority over the masses who thoughtlessly continue with their meat diet. In fact, some very evil people have been vegetarians; Adolf Hitler is a prime example.

Nevertheless, the gross exploitation of animals for the gluttonous feeding of humans is unpleasant to consider; these humans inhabit the developed countries and are too materialistically inclined already. The starving millions elsewhere in the world would, like the Prodigal Son, be glad to fill their bellies with the pods that the pigs were eating. Albert Schweitzer's dictum of "reverence for life" seems the noblest compromise. "Nature red in tooth and claw" does not exclude the human, who also has to live out his allotted span in order to do the work appointed for him. But what he is obliged to kill, whether for food or scientific research, should be treated with deep concern and caused as little distress as possible. No creature can escape death, but its life should be as fulfilled as is commensurate with its biological status. The prodigality of nature is itself phenomenal, presumably an attempt to ensure the survival of at least some members of the group in the face of the hazards facing all of them. I like Albert Schweitzer's prayer, "O heavenly father, protect and bless all things that have breath, guard them from all evil and let them sleep in peace."

# 7

# The Making of a Person

The creation of a human starts in the mother's womb; it proceeds through childhood and adolescence when it appears to have its fulfilment at the time of "coming of age". The individual is now an adult and can use the power within him, refined by education, to do the work set in front of him. The results of this potency we have already considered: abuse of nature, internecine strife and death. Natural man has unlimited powers of creativity but something always seems to go wrong. It is here that the biblical narrative casts illumination on the mundane scene.

The history of God's ancient people the Jews falls into three well-defined epochs. First there is the deliverance from Egyptian slavery under the prophetic leadership of Moses. For the first time in their experience the chosen people taste freedom and a limited degree of power. Despite their frequent backslidings, which tempt Moses himself to some obscure denial of God's supremacy and his ultimate demotion by the Almighty to merely seeing the promised land from afar, they reach their destination under the leadership of Moses' adjutant Joshua. There they are installed through the favour of God. Almost at once they apostatize, and experience repeated periods of slavery to the local tribes until delivered by various judges appointed by God. The pattern of enslavement, deliverance, apostasy, and further defeat and slavery persists until the time of the prophet Samuel and the beneficent King David. Under him there is a union of the two kingdoms of Israel and Judah, and the people do seem to have attained a semblance of national identity. Indeed, the conclusion of the Second Book of Samuel and the beginning of the First Book of Kings, which recounts the wisdom of David's son Solomon, is the high point of ancient Hebrew history.

The later backsliding of Solomon under the influence of his numerous foreign wives and concubines sees the separation of the two kingdoms, and, with occasional periods of genuine reform and religious fervour, there is a gradual descent to a much more radical defeat by the Assyrians, who deport the people of the northern kingdom of Israel so that they disappear from the pages of history, while the southern kingdom of Judah is miraculously saved. However, its preservation is only temporary, for the degeneracy of most of its kings ensures that it too is destroyed, this time by the Babylonians, who carry most of the population into exile. Fortunately the Babylonians prove to be much more benign captors, and under them the exiles thrive and grow in spirituality. The Persian prophet Zoroaster whom we have already mentioned probably played some part in this awakening. And then, miraculously once more, the

Persian conqueror of the Babylonians, Cyrus, is inspired to send the exiles back to Palestine to rebuild their temple and start their lives afresh under their ancient law. And so the brash potency of the original people of Israel is tempered by experience and civilized by suffering as a precious remnant returns to rebuild on a life restored and humbled by the divine grace.

The Jews, as they may now justly be called especially after the teaching work of Ezra, who dissolves all foreign marriages in order to ensure the purity of the religion (thereby reversing the trend to apostasy witnessed especially by Solomon), grow slowly in spiritual obedience to God, but, until our own time, are not to know political independence again. The Persians are followed by the Greeks, who also leave their impress on Judaism, and then come the Romans. On the whole, the people are left alone to continue their own tradition (the Hellenizing intolerance of Antiochus Epiphanes and the necessary reaction of the Jews is an exception, and fully recounted in the two Books of Maccabees). In their mind looms the figure of the Messiah who is to set them free, long ago prophesied by Isaiah, Micah and Zechariah.

The initial period of liberation is thus followed by the second period of restoration. And then comes the third period. The Messiah does indeed come, but he is unrecognized by his compatriots. They looked for a national redeemer, but instead the Suffering Servant of Isaiah 53 makes his appearance. The

Prince of Peace is no help to the Zealots, while his effortless integrity puts the traditional doctors of the law to shame, but his spiritual gifts place him in a category of excellence far beyond that of any person, let alone religious party. They know inwardly that he is the one sent and yet they refuse to believe it, because the inner revolution such an admission would entail is beyond human imagination. The words of John 1:10–12 ring eternally true, "He was in the world; but the world, though it owed its being to him, did not recognize him. He entered his own realm, and his own would not receive him. But to all who did receive him, to those who have yielded him their allegiance, he gave the right to become children of God." This is the test; it does not depend on historical claims or theological disputation (for how, logically, can God become human! Or, as John says in 1:14, "the Word became flesh; he came to dwell among us, and we saw his glory, such glory as befits the Father's only Son, full of grace and truth"). In the Word we come to the full knowledge of God, attaining the state of deification as far as mortal human can rise to the divine being. And as we ascend the ladder of spiritual perfection, which is an intimate knowledge of God, so the mysteries of the Incarnation become clearer to our minds. In other words, we know by participation rather than by distant analysis. The third period, preceded as we remember by liberation and restoration, is glorification.

Jesus is the proper man, or as St Irenaeus says,

"The glory of God is a man fully alive." Neither the Jews as people nor humanity at large have attained this stage of development. This includes those who have accepted the messiahship of Jesus and his deity, and call themselves Christians. While the Jews have erred in not accepting Jesus, the Christians have erred just as grievously in not following his example. The shameful record of the Christian Church cannot be denied; its cruelty both to non-believers and to deviant members within its own ranks is a black mark of history. And yet it has been the principal agent of civilizing the world and redressing social injustice (by contrast, the religions of India and China have been so concerned with ultimate states of being that they scandalously neglected the material needs of large masses of their people until the time of Western penetration some centuries ago). In fact, a more mature consideration of the history of the Christian faith makes the dark episodes more comprehensible. Under the vision of God nothing can remain concealed. To fall into the hands of the Living God is a terrible experience, for all secrets lie revealed in their naked loathsomeness. But once they are acknowledged in honest humility, the means of their healing are ensured. It is this lack of honesty and refusal to give ourselves freely in our moral baseness to God that prevents our ascent to the realm of Christ's stature. We are, as St Paul says, saved by God's grace, through trusting him, and not by our own efforts. It is God's gift, and not a reward for work done. There is nothing for anyone to boast of (Ephesians 2:8–9).

With this model in mind we can trace the creation of a full person. The youth with his vigour and education leaves home to make his way in the world. If he follows his natural bent, he will probably, in one way or another, follow the footsteps of the Prodigal Son, ending up in some sort of plight. Indeed, if he were to stay the course in a life of pure self-gratification, though he might outwardly appear enviable to those who never seem to have made the grade, he would be a most unfortunate individual. Though filled with outer riches, he would find increasingly with the advent of ageing that he had nothing permanent to call his own. All there would be were sad memories of a youthful past, tantalizingly unattainable in his present circumstances. Let it be insisted at once that this picture of the heedless materialist does not decry the importance of worldly success or belittle the value of pleasure in the growth of a person; those who sneer at life's good things usually have been unable personally to attain them, just as those who suspect the motives of altruistic people are usually those of poor achievement in their own careers. Until an individual has received some recognition of his own unique place in society, he has hardly begun to value himself. This substantiation should come from his own family, but often this is not forthcoming, and a piece of good fortune or unexpected pleasure may act as a source of inner illumination.

Nevertheless, self-affirmation that depends on material success and good fortune is like the house

Jesus describes at the end of the Sermon on the Mount: built on sand and therefore vulnerable to the assaults of the weather. In due course tragedy will strike the comfortable edifice of the materialist, and this is his moment of growth into an expanded consciousness of reality. The liberation of the young person from the tutelage of his elders has at some time to progress to a restoration of security but under the aegis of God rather than material circumstances.

And yet God himself can become a type of idol preventing the individual's full development. Some people have a intuitive awareness of God that gives them great strength, but if they depend too heavily on the relationship they may not grow into full maturity. An essential part of their spiritual journey may entail forfeiting that assurance so that they are able to stand on their own without any additional support. However, if the relationship is real it will stay the course in dark faith both in the glare of worldly scepticism and the gloom of personal tragedy. The relationship is real when it seeks no recompense or looks for anything outside itself. It is, as it were, a union of the frail individual with the weakness of God that Bonhoeffer wrote about as part of our true coming of age, not as striplings full of our own prowess but as responsible people deeply involved in the suffering world. This is the way of approach of the seeker who has voluntarily or by force of events come to God in his eternal mode as the ground of being, in whom we live and move and have our existence (Acts 17:28). He is never far from us, but we have to grow into his presence before we can do the great work ahead of us. This is the attainment of full personhood.

This same critique of God is true of revivalistic techniques that play on the emotions of sick people, stressing the punitive nature of God, but assuring free pardon once they make their submission to him (and the evangelistic team whose zeal makes them automatically partners in the divine exercise). This type of God can be freely manipulated, while at the same time he manipulates us by offering us good things while we are obedient to him and his helpers, but threatening us with dire punishment if we fail to do what he commands, as interpreted by a particular approach to scripture or the verbal inspiration of a person claiming prophetic status.

Another great prophet of our century, Martin Buber, in his classic *I and Thou* has come close to the essence of the self. He writes, "When *Thou* is spoken, the speaker has no thing for his object. For where there is a thing there is another thing. Every *It* is bounded by others: *It* exists only through being bounded by others. But when *Thou* is spoken, there is no thing. *Thou* has no bounds. When *Thou* is spoken, the speaker has no *thing*; he is indeed nothing. But he takes his stand in relation.' He also writes, "As experience, the world belongs to the primary word *I-It*. The primary word *I-Thou* establishes the world of relation." Penetrating the deepest mysteries of creation may bring a mastery with it, but it

110

excludes the relationship which is true knowledge, like the knowledge of husband and wife that precedes the conception of a great soul in the biblical narrative. In the same way, an obsessive straining after the gifts of the Holy Spirit can prevent us coming close to God; the more we seek to please him, the more does the ego separate us from him. The conception of chosen souls in the Bible is the presage of a creation that goes beyond personal desire to communal service, beyond sectarian loyalty to universal compassion, beyond utilitarian concern to a burning love for all that exists. This is the creativity of a spiritually mature person as compared with the facile virtuosity of the brash youngster recently come of age.

The making of a person is intimately related to his apprehension of the deep things of existence. His approach to his Creator determines his own place in the scheme of reality. In the early phase of liberation he may have to lose the God whose beneficent presence had formerly supported him, who could be manipulated under the guise of prayer and worship. Such a God is an *It*, whom we know at best in terms of the results of prayer and worship. It is with deepening self-knowledge that we come closer to the true God, who is a *Thou* closer to our essence than our own awareness of him may be.

How then do we come to this deepened self-knowledge? The more it is sought, the more surely does it elude one. Personal acquisitiveness separates us from true relationship, converting a *Thou* to an *It*.

In the beautiful Wisdom poem of Job 28, we are told that only right living and an awe of the Creator can lead us to true wisdom as opposed to specialized knowledge. This right living is not a formula, nor can it be learned in secret schools devoted to the occult dimension. We remember Buber's distinction between the experience of *It* and the relationship inherent in *Thou*. He writes, "I experience something. If we add 'secret' to 'open' experiences, nothing in the situation is changed. How self-confident is that wisdom which perceives a closed compartment in things, reserved for the initiate and manipulated only with the key. O secrecy without a secret! O accumulation of information! *It*, always *It*!"

The authentic spring of self-knowledge comes from a crisis in which the customary supports have been stripped away from the individual; these include not only the superficial appurtenances of wealth and possessions but frequently also health, friends and even religious convictions. The Job story is typical, and indeed this particular writing can never fade into obscurity while the human remains as he is. All that remains is a silence that overwhelms by its finality. Bonhoeffer rightly insists that we should find God in the totality of life, not only during the periods of pain. However, until we are brought low, we have no time to listen and to hear amid the din of worldly distractions, which can easily include ritual religious observances performed as an insurance against future misfortune (the spectre of Job before his calamities comes to mind here). In the lives of most people suffering renders the mind more open to wisdom from sources both within itself (from the unconscious realms where the intuition dwells) and from outside (from the teachings of others who have experienced the authentic Spirit of God in various adverse circumstances). The lack of awareness so typical of the human condition requires an inner jolt for the individual to awaken and hear the One who knocks unceasingly at the door of the soul. He is usually kept waiting because we have "better" things to do.

The type of God who is a punishing *It* has to be eclipsed before the embracing *Thou* of reality is fully known. A profound knowledge of God may follow the descent of a heedless person into "a valley dark as death" (Psalm 23:4) as he battles for life in the intensive therapy unit of a hospital. Apart from the rather special near-death experience we have already mentioned in considering the relationship between the mind and the brain, the previously selfish man of the world, whose life revolved around money, food and sex, may come to a deeper appreciation of reality as he witnesses the unceasing concern for his survival of a life-support team. The selfless service of the medical personnel throws the indulgence of his past way of life into sharp relief, just as his present helplessness brings with it a sober appraisal of his situation as he now has to face it. What indeed does it profit one whose life is in peril even if one has attained a pinnacle of worldly success? At first the battle for survival will occupy his attention, but as he gets better, so may a more chastened view of reality appear. For the first time in his life he may feel gratitude, primarily to those who attended him but more distantly to the nameless presence who stood by him as in the wings of a theatre. This presence slowly moves the centre of his existence from the ego as an end in itself to its place as servant, the same servant who washed the feet of his disciples the night he was betrayed into the power of sinful people. This slow relation to the embracing *Thou* is a much more profound knowledge of God than the unsure experience of a judgemental *It*, as may be encountered in a state of religious enthusiasm. The embracing God neither demands or expects and nor does the person, because the relationship is the gift and the presence the proof of eternity.

At last we have a knowledge of God as the source of life, the ground of being, who is also the lover who leaves his beloved to work out his own salvation in awe and responsibility, so that in the end the two may meet in a friendship that far outdistances any human tie in its constancy and eternity. As Buber puts it, "All real living is meeting." In this relationship the springs of human creativity have been fully tapped. It is the creative contact with the Deity that sets in motion the power of imagining and the concentration of thought that starts a new cycle of human endeavour. No longer is the human in control – indeed, the very notion of control or domination is out of place – but instead he is the servant who brings joy to his fellows and healing to the entire created order. As he grows in the life of silent communion which we call prayer, so he can tap into a reservoir of inspiration as infinite as God himself. It is, in fact, the Holy Spirit that is met, the person of the Godhead who infuses life into all that exists by virtue of his ceaseless love.

"Remember your Creator in the days of your youth, before the time of trouble comes and the years draw near when you will say, 'I see no purpose in them'. Remember him before the sun and the light of day give place to darkness" (Ecclesiastes 12:1–2). This seems to be the heart of the matter. The writer of Ecclesiastes has no illusions about the transience of happiness, the vagaries of fortune, the vanity of human achievement and the finality of death. He has no certainty of personal survival to comfort him, and his honesty is chilling though peculiarly refreshing. But he does seem to be saying that God, though obscure to human understanding, is a real companion in a dark course. He alone can illuminate the dark stretches of existence, for he is constant when everything else fails. He is not a God who fills in the gaps of our ignorance; he is the source of all that exists. Though he does not invade our privacy, he is always at hand to share our burdens and clear the portals of our perception and understanding so that we may proceed better with our life's work. In the action of prayer we draw close to him, his Spirit infuses our own spirit, and we approach more closely the image in which we were created.

The process is prolonged, in my opinion going far beyond any mortal lifetime. A dramatic religious conversion is sometimes an important landmark on the way, and those committed to evangelization do the Lord's work provided they learn to trust God in his transactions with those whom they have brought to him. The problem with revivalistic groups is that they do not trust God fully. Therefore they are psychologically bound to the forces of destruction even when they affirm the victory of God over the devil. We have to learn to let go, not only of the things of this world but also of the people closest to us. The model of the father of the Prodigal Son is important here. He believed in his heart that the Holy Spirit would eventually lead his headstrong son home, and meanwhile he remembered him. This is the basis of intercessory prayer, not so much asking as never ceasing to remember in love.

Jesus himself had to depart before the full power of the Holy Spirit could come to action in his disciples (John 16:7). While he remained with them, they would simply have rested in his authority and done nothing themselves. Only during their bereavement did they begin to know themselves in their naked wretchedness, and the period of their restoration followed the forgiveness of their resurrected Master. They were at last growing into full personhood, and their understanding of God matured from an *It* that could be relied on for favours to a *Thou* with whom they had a constant relationship. This *Thou* was the risen Christ whom they knew as a person and also

God the Son who showed them the full measure of the Father.

Every experience on the path helps us on the way provided we stay awake and learn from each moment as it passes us by. To be a realized person is to create in the shadow of God.

# 8

## The Priesthood of Humanity

When we consider the whole evolutionary process in its panoramic intensity, we see a gradually unfolding emergence of intelligence from the humble forms of living organisms with the human as the apex of a climactic ascent. At last a focus of consciousness has emerged that can cooperate rationally with the creative process. The human was created in the image of the supreme Creator whom we may call God, so that he might lift up the world from the mortality inherent in matter to the immortality, indeed the eternity, of spirit. Physicists have pondered long over the remarkable purposefulness of creation, how, from the "big bang" 15,000 million years ago the wonderful drama of evolving species has unfolded, culminating in the marvel of human intelligence. It seems clear to many of them who would not disport religious sentiments that a higher purpose must surely have been at work that this remarkable series of events occurring over many millions of years should have attained its climax in human development, which itself is not complete. This insight is the basis of the "anthropic principle", for animal and especially human development could not have occurred in an arbitrary universe.

And yet nothing is foreordained so tightly that free will is bypassed or rendered inoperative. Just as even the most promising person may squander his gifts in vice so that his life is ruined, so may humanity at large destroy both itself and the earth if it behaves outrageously. In this respect it may be argued that only one small planet would then go up in smoke, but deeper intuitive awareness tells us that small as we are, we are all parts of a greater body of life that includes the universe itself. This "panpsychism" offends many of rigid scientific discipline as also those religious groups that frown on mysticism with its tacit universalistic tendencies (hoping that in the end all creation will be saved and that hell will not be eternal), but as we mount the ladder of prayer, so are we brought in contact with a world beyond our small compass. Intercession depends on this principle, but the realm of creation is greater than our limited personal concerns. In the divine presence nothing is separate from our concern any more than God's love can be excluded from any of his creatures. The creature may, and often does, withdraw, but the love does not wane, for love will never come to an end, as St Paul writes in 1 Corinthians 13:8.

It seems unlikely that the creation of the human being with his enormous cerebral capacity, sufficient, as it were, to accommodate a soul that not only thinks under exigencies and plans for emergencies but also grasps in its radiance a larger vision of life in which

119

freedom and joy may prevail, was a chance event. The human has his feet on the earth but his head is in the heavens. He is able to make a conscious contact with the Creator, and can therefore think heavenly thoughts and literally bring heaven to earth. But his carnal nature tends towards self-preservation, which soon encroaches on the lives of his weaker brethren as the lust for power and possessions dominates his thoughts. The human is therefore a spiritual animal, and both components of his nature have to be given due respect: without the body he is no use to the world, but without the spirit his intellectual capacity would be destructive to all creation. In this respect we remember Jesus' diagnosis of his disciples' condition after their poor showing at Gethsemane, "The spirit is willing but the flesh is weak" (Mark 14:38). We have already considered the slow, yet dramatic, process whereby a mature person is created, and how this process is intimately involved in his relationship with the Creator who can no longer be an *It* to manipulate but becomes a *Thou* in whom to rest in friendship. Only then do the divine and human wills come into juxtaposition so that the one does not dominate the other. Instead they serve one another. If the thought of God serving man seems outrageous, we should recall Jesus' statement, "For even the Son of Man did not come to be served but to serve, and to give up his life as a ransom for many" (Mark 10:45).

This mention of a ransom brings us to the most profound conception of human activity in the world, that of priesthood. As we read in Leviticus 4:5–6, under the Law of Moses a priest was one commissioned to offer up sacrifices for his own sins and those of the people. In addition, he taught the people and prayed for them; his consecration and ordination were of God. The sacrifice was of animals, and up to Jesus' day the dealers in pigeons and the money-changers had a legitimate place in the temple. Jesus' strong-handed action in expelling them all was not a condemnation of their trade but a comment on the way their cupidity, inevitable where commerce is involved, had polluted the atmosphere of the temple. "My house shall be called a house of prayer for all the nations, but you have made it a robbers' den", is the way Mark 11:17 puts it. It is noteworthy that the chief priests and doctors of the law were not grateful for Jesus' intervention, but sought a way of getting rid of him, an action not uncommon when an established clergy is criticized by someone more obviously God-centred than they.

However, there was a deeper meaning to Jesus' violent action. It, like the equally disturbing cursing of the barren fig tree, was a symbolic action. It proclaimed the time when sacrifice would be internal and spiritual rather than external and manipulative. The cursing of the fig tree proclaimed the end of institutions that had ceased to serve a useful function and were merely parasitic on the common resources. The talents, to quote Jesus' parable of Matthew 25: 14–30, are there to be used profitably; if they are not, they are distributed to those who are worthy while

121

the incompetent servant is immediately dismissed. The story of evolution is a universal illustration of this truth.

Christ indeed came to inaugurate a new priesthood; the concept was not altered but the means were refined and spiritualized. In the great Letter to the Hebrews, one indeed of priestly magnitude, Christ is compared with Melchizedek the mysterious king of Salem who was a priest of God Most High, who blessed Abraham and to whom in turn the patriarch gave a tithe of all the booty he had taken in a local skirmish (Genesis 14:18–20). He is compared in Hebrews 7:3 to the Son of God, and he remains a priest for all time. His priesthood is of another order to that conferred on Levi and his descendants, for he lives on whereas they, mere mortals, live only an apportioned span. In Hebrews 9:11–12 the priesthood of Christ is seen to be not merely of the universe, which is finite, but of eternity. Furthermore, the blood of sacrifice is not secondhand from various animals but his own blood. And so he has entered the sanctuary once and for all and secured an eternal deliverance. By contrast, the high priest of the old dispensation had the privilege of entering into the sanctuary once a year, on the Day of Atonement, to make expiation for the sins of the whole people (Leviticus 16 describes the matter in detail). In Hebrews 9:24 we come to the conclusion of the matter, "For Christ has entered, not that sanctuary made by men's hands which is only a symbol of the

122

reality, but heaven itself, to appear now before God on our behalf".

In the person of the proper man, God was reconciling the world to himself. As Christ took on the sin of the world and gave it to God, so was humanity (and by extension the whole world) brought into a new relationship with reality, no longer dominated by the bodily nature that looks for rewards and is not ashamed to hurt other creatures for its own comfort, but inspired to look for universal healing in the power of the human spirit now fully illuminated by the Holy Spirit of God. A new vision of wholeness has been revealed, and the dignity as well as the spiritual potentiality of the human, already felt intuitively by the earliest members of the species *Homo*, had come truly of age. However, as we have already stated, the stature of Jesus remains unfulfilled in human nature. Apart from that select body of saints that adorn the annals of humanity – and these belong to all the great religious and cultural groups, by no means confined to those who claim a Christian allegiance – people are still largely unawakened to the potentialities for transformation lying deep within them. As Meister Eckhart and Angelus Silesius would insist, the birth of Christ in the individual soul is even more important than the birth of Jesus in Bethlehem. Nevertheless, the Incarnation has shown us the full union of humanity and Deity, and it is to this that we must work day by day in the honest pursuance of our particular calling.

The human acts as an intermediary. He stretches

123

to God in his spirit and touches the earth in his body. His work is to bring down the divine splendour to the earth, at the same time lifting up the world to God, from whom alone healing and renewal can come. This is a priestly function, as yet mediated only by a professional priesthood, some of whom are still unaware of the privilege they have and the great sacrifice expected of them. In the old dispensation the sacrificial animal sufficed, but after the Incarnation and all that followed, it became clear that Christ alone could do the great work of reconciliation. But now he lives in the hearts of all true believers, and they too have the responsibility of sacrifice thrust upon them. Of no one is this more true than the priest, whose life is consecrated (set aside for or dedicated) to God. This consecration is a divine act, but the human must first give of himself wholeheartedly. It is a terrible thing to fall into the hands of the Living God, for now our very being is under the closest scrutiny and everything unclean and perverse is brought into the open, at least of our own awareness, prior to its slow, painful, progressive and total healing. Attitudes and drives that would have been quite natural in the lower animals have to be spiritualized: while we are alive we cannot disregard the various demands of the body for nourishment, shelter and procreation (if one is not in celibate vows), but we have to be their master and no longer their slave. In this way the spirit infuses the body while being incarnate within its hospitable bounds.

The way by which this purification is achieved is a combination of prayer, communal worship and service to the larger community. Priesthood embraces all three even if the first two would seem to be the more "professional" side of the work. Prayer brings the person to the divine presence; worship pays homage to God in the midst of a believing community, while service brings down the divine power and love to the whole world. As Christ would say, "You, like the lamp, must shed your light among your fellows, so that, when they see the good you do, they may give praise to your Father in heaven" (Matthew 5:16).

It is in the sphere of prayer and worship that the religions of India and China, earlier on criticized for striving after ultimate states of being while large numbers of their people were living in penury, can be of great value to the West. The stress of Hinduism, Buddhism and Taoism on the inner way of progress is a salutory corrective to the excessive activity of the technological age. The Christian Church sometimes falls victim to an "activism" of extreme social works to the considerable exclusion of the inner way in an attempt to come to terms with the noisy, unreflecting world outside. The Far East has accepted the material benefits of Western civilization, and now quite a few thoughtful Westerners are exploring the depth of the spiritual realm by the practice of meditation techniques acquired from Eastern sources. Thus an encounter with the saints of Indian religion may illuminate insights of Christian spirituality that have been obscured by the formal dogmatism of theologians and ministers who have given little of their time to the practice of prayer. The more God is discussed, the further does his presence recede from us. The *It* of discursive meditation becomes the all-embracing *Thou* of God when we leave discussion behind and enter the silence of the present moment.

Just as the priest brings the blessing of God to the people and lifts up their sins to God, in the process offering himself as a sacrifice on the altar in imitation of his Lord, so is the human to bring the benefits of his chastened intellect to the world. While this entails scientific enlightenment that seeks to eradicate disease and rectify the results of past misdemeanours that have so damaged the natural order, there must also be a love sufficient for the person to sacrifice his very life for creation. By his action he erases the world's stain that he himself has created in no small measure. He lifts the world's agony to God, and his sacrifice initiates a reaction of world transformation. In Psalm 51:17 we read, "My sacrifice, O God, is a broken spirit; a wounded heart, O God, thou will not despise." God accepts this more readily than any material gift because it comes from the person directly. When Abraham was preparing to sacrifice his son Isaac to God, a substitute ram appeared in the thicket, whereas Jesus' sacrifice was absolute. Through the mediation and example of the proper man we too have to make the great sacrifice as we enter upon our sombre yet glorious priesthood of the Universal Church, which is the entirety of the universe. It is admittedly condensed into our little earth, but it is in psychic communion with the cosmos, that vast realm which includes the universe and the intermediate mental/psychic/spiritual dimension.

The enigma of moral existence is the prevalence of evil. This is something more than the suffering inherent in evolution itself, remembering that the world no less than its inhabitants is in a state of growth and its fabric is unstable, liable to natural disasters of various types. Evil, unlike natural suffering, has a moral component. While "nature red in tooth and claw" simply strives for its own survival, the evil impulse in the human works relentlessly for the downfall of his fellow creatures, often with a savage delight in the cruelty involved. Evil is never satisfied. The brutality of genocide, a number of examples of which have disfigured our technologically advanced century, emphasizes these qualities dramatically. Evil as a moral entity comes into existence only when its victim can appreciate its injustice and seek redress in some court of higher law. It is possible that highly domesticated animals can share their owners' repugnance inasmuch as they have absorbed something of the human soul consciousness.

It is very probable that the source of evil lies in the mental/psychic/spiritual realm that we touched on at the beginning of our reflections. Here work the angelic hierarchy; the good are messengers of the light of the Holy Spirit, while the debased are messengers of the evil one whom we call the devil, probably a fallen angel of immense power. All this is, of course, conjectural except to those who are psychically sensitive. Such people are especially vulnerable to assault by the dark forces but are also of enormous potential use in the conflict with evil, the rescue of endangered individuals, and ultimately the cleansing of this vast, immaterial realm which is an intermediate dimension between the divine mind and the human imagination. The origin of the perverse impulse is a mystery, but a likely explanation is the result of the free will granted the Creator to his rational creatures, which would, according to this line of argument, include the angelic hosts as well as the human being.

It would seem that the human is the intermediary for both God and the devil. The human intellect is morally neutral, capable of use for unashamed self-gratification or world service, calculated genocide or re-creation of the world free from ignorance and injustice. If one looks dispassionately at the source of the evil impulse in one's own being, one will often find insecurity very close to the surface. While one is insecure in one's own identity, one will tend to covet the riches of this world to complement one's own lack in the belief that wealth, power, or social standing are the keys to personal fulfilment and happiness. Not only will one grasp at these in the round of daily existence but one will also envy others who appear to possess them. Envy acts as a cancer of the soul, for it dominates the attention to the exclusion of more profitable concerns. As the obsession grows, so the person will shrink at nothing to realize his desires, while the seething malice within him will work to the destruction of anyone standing in his way. Murder becomes justifiable to a deranged mind which can project the person's own base motives onto the life-style or beliefs of his victim.

While this perverse psychological process is developing inwardly, the person is unwittingly connected to the demonic sources in the intermediate mental/psychic/spiritual realm. He may be used as an instrument of fearful destruction far greater than anything he imagined even in the worst frenzies of his hatred. Some deranged people actually ally themselves to the devil much as a more normal individual would pay service to the powers of light, whether or not he confessed a religious allegiance. Satanism is not rare nowadays, but its practitioners are invariably swallowed up in the evil they have mixed with through their departure from the decencies of life.

The question inevitably arises: are we in control of our lives or are we merely the playthings of vast forces using us for their own ends? Since free will is the precious gift of the Creator to his rational creature, we must accept that he alone is responsible for his actions. But he does not live in isolation. If he chooses the way of life he aligns his will to that of the Creator, but if he chooses death (not only for himself but for any other creature except in circumstances of the greatest exigency such as self-defence or self-preservation in respect of killing animals for food), he works hand in hand with the forces of darkness. Buber writes, "The primary word *I-It* is not of evil – as matter is not evil. It is of evil – as matter is, which presumes to have the quality of present being. If a man lets it have the mastery, the continually growing world of *It* overruns him and robs him of the quality of his own *I*, till the incubus over him and the ghost within him whisper to one another the confession of their non-salvation." In other words, while our sights are limited to the world of matter and our own physical satisfaction, we are in dangerous relationship with the forces of darkness. On the other hand, however, if we avoid all worldly temptations ("the world, the flesh and the devil"), we make no contact with matter, and our lives, though harmless, are also ineffectual both to ourselves and to the world. Security in fact comes from the Creator alone: when we rest in him we are truly safe, needing nothing else to substantiate our identity while being available to do whatever circumstances decree, without either fear or bombast.

This is both the dilemma and the glory of human priesthood. We are of the world and yet not confined by it, for our spirit inhabits eternity. In the words of Isaiah 57:15, "Thus speaks the high and exalted one, whose name is holy, who lives for ever: I dwell in a high and holy place with him who is broken and humble in spirit, to revive the spirit of the humble, to revive the courage of the broken." We are close to the Creator God but are not ourselves divine; at the most there is a spark of divinity within the spirit of the soul. This spark has to burst forth to a glowing fire. The seed of Christ within has to germinate and grow into the full tree of life. We are here to lift up mortal nature to immortal radiance when we realize our priesthood in calm responsibility. But we can as easily act as priests for the demonic forces when we elevate our own interests above the good of the world. The choice is ours. Even if we choose a divine priesthood there is no infallible set of rules. St Paul comes as near the truth as anyone when he states that love cannot wrong a neighbour, therefore the whole law is summed up in love (Romans 13:10).

The problem here is the real meaning of love. Human love extends from heroic self-sacrifice to lust masquerading as affection. It is often strongly manipulative, the beloved invariably, as Buber laments, slipping from a *Thou* to an *It*. Therefore we learn to love properly from the Creator, who loved us first. Human affection and concern are reflections of this creative love, but they inevitably have their limits which are those of the flesh in its native weakness. Love is not primarily an emotion; it is an energy, a power, indeed, the very power of the Holy Spirit pouring down upon us. It does not look for acknowledgment or results because it is both cause and result. We learn the secret of love in silence when we are open to the downflow of the Holy Spirit upon our own spirit. At that moment Christ is born in us, the spark bursts into flame, and the seed puts out its first shoot.

The strange course of our earthly life is to bring us to a fulfilment of our priesthood. The encounter with evil is as important in the development of our personality as are our times of heavenly communion, for it is only thus that we can grow in experience while at the same time playing our part in lifting up matter to spirit. Just as Jesus offended the pillars of respectability by consorting with the dregs of society, so we too have to suffer many things, experience many disturbing emotions and encounter many temptations. It is noteworthy that the "good" people who detest all they regard as unclean are somewhat closer to the powers of darkness than are the less exalted members of society. This is because their very moral stringency can serve to occlude the deeper springs of compassion and love, such as the Creator has for his creatures. On the other hand, those who pride themselves on their liberal tolerance, by downgrading moral standards in the service of compassion for the deviant members of society, can also become agents of darkness when their concern for the underdog conceals a deeper hatred of "the establishment".

Wherever there is an underlying hatred we may be quite sure that the demonic forces lurk, waiting patiently for the moment when they can explode into violence and cause general destruction. Both moral principles and liberal tolerance will rapidly go up in smoke, as the events of our century show us all too clearly. Compared with this, the efforts of occultists pale into insignificance in the evil they may produce.

The priest, elevating the elements of the Eucharist,

brings consecrated matter to God, who in turn gives of himself to the congregation as they receive the bread and the wine. The very body of Christ is now within them. The remainder of both priest's and congregation's lives is devoted to their growing sanctity, which must flow out to embrace all people, indeed all creation. As they grow in their own darkness, so they see the light more distinctly. As they know their own humiliation, so they can participate more understandingly in the mortification of the world as it "groans in all its parts as if in the pangs of childbirth" (Romans 8:22). In this way, following the vocation of the professional priest, humanity is raised up to God so that its own priesthood may be established and fulfilled. "You shall be my kingdom of priests, my holy nation" (Exodus 19:6). These words spoken by Moses as God's prophet to the Israelites were brought a stage nearer fulfilment for all people by the advent of Christ, but until the Creator Spirit is fully upon and within them, they cannot perform the great work of healing the universe.

# 9

# The Consummation of All Things

Material creation commenced with an enormous explosion 15,000 million years ago, so the cosmologists inform us. They also prognosticate an end of the universe some time, probably millions of years, in the future. As John Polkinghorne in his authoritative book *Science and Creation* reminds us, the universe's future looks bleak; its history from the moment of the "big bang" onwards has been a conflict between two opposing tendencies: an explosive force throwing matter apart and the force of gravity pulling matter together. At present they are closely balanced but we cannot assume this state of affairs will continue indefinitely. The dominance of either of these tendencies will put paid to the structure of the universe. Therefore the death of the physical body in store for all living forms has its more sombre counterpart in the destruction of the universe at some indeterminate time in the future.

A consideration of the remarkable events that followed Jesus' death on the cross may illuminate this dark future in store for matter generally. Jesus' body, according to the witness of the gospel writers, disappeared unaccountably from the tomb, but from the third day after his crucifixion until the time of his ascension forty days afterwards, his physical form was seen by numerous disciples on various occasions. That form was not the same as the body of the earthly Jesus, for even his closest friends did not recognize him until he gave some gesture or said something that, as it were, opened the eyes of the people around him. And then he tended to disappear from their midst. The very contradictory nature of some of the appearances vouches more profoundly for their validity than would a carefully doctored account that smoothed out all the unaccountable elements. Above all, those who witnessed the appearances were not only convinced of Jesus' survival but, even more important, were themselves moved from despair to certainty. They were in their own way as resurrected as was their Lord, so that a mission that appeared to be a terrible failure in terms of the crucifixion turned out to be a glorious vindication of their dearest expectations.

As in Adam all men die, so in Christ all will be brought to life (1 Corinthians 15: 22). The death and disintegration of the physical body of our allegorical ancestor Adam is reversed by the advent of the fully actualized man Jesus. The spiritual radiance of Christ shown to three of his disciples at the time of the transfiguration came to its full glory after the crucifixion, when the disfigured physical body was so filled with God's uncreated light that it became spontaneously spiritualized. This process was completed at the time of the ascension. In the resurrection period of forty days the presence of Jesus effected a deep relationship with all who were open to his love. In the mental/psychic/spiritual realm he was in direct contact with saints and sinners, angels and their demonic counterpart. This was an aspect of the descent into hell mentioned in the so-called Apostles' Creed; in fact, it started immediately after Jesus' death. But it was also an ascent to paradise where the blessed spirits dwelt, and where Jesus promised the repentant thief on the cross he would be with him that very day. After the ascension Christ returned to his original place in mystical eternity with the Father and the Holy Spirit, in the process taking the physical nature of the universe and the quality of humanity with him.

All this may seem very remote from everyday concerns in this life, but it provides a presage, a foretaste, of things to come when death is finally overcome in victory. The first man, Adam, became an animate being, whereas the last Adam has become a life-giving spirit (1 Corinthians 15:45). While we are limited to material things we are bound to death. As we open ourselves to spiritual truth, so does eternity permeate our earthly concerns. This is not a process of lifting ourselves above the demands of earthly life (which would be a subtle way of escape from our immediate duties), but rather bringing down the Holy Spirit on all we do each moment in our mundane toil. St Paul writes, "The created universe waits with eager expectation for God's sons to be revealed. It was made the victim of frustration, not by its own choice, but because of him who made it so; yet always there was hope, because the universe itself is to be freed from the shackles of mortality and enter upon the liberty and splendour of the children of God. Up to the present, we know, the whole created universe groans in all its parts as if in the pangs of childbirth". (Romans 8:19–22). In this gloriously inspired vision he goes on to write that even we who have been given the Holy Spirit as first fruits of the harvest to come are groaning inwardly while we await God's action in making us his sons and setting our whole body free. Through Christ we have indeed been saved, though only in hope.

A new depth of understanding, a greater participation in the life of the universe, was opened to humanity in the ministry and sacrificial death of Christ, in whom the Creator worked to reconcile the world to himself. To those who confessed the name of Christ came the first understanding of the new dispensation effected by the life of their Master, but the fruits of this dispensation have overflowed to the world at large. We have to face the fact that the early effects can be frightening in their stripping from us of all illusions of health and decency; in God all things lie revealed. It is in this way that our salvation seems a long way off as we have to confront all the base impulses within ourselves. But if we proceed with humility and courage, the light will shine within us as the spark of divinity in the soul is able to burst forth into a gentle flame that gathers momentum once the inner atmosphere becomes clearer and less polluted by the vice of the world.

This is the way of the saints of humanity. What they reveal is our way of ascent also. Whenever we perform an action of selfless service (being selfless it is so spontaneous that the ego falls into line and serves instead of premeditating what is most expedient for its own benefit), we are helping to raise up the world to that immortality that St Paul envisages. And in so doing we enter more fully into the sonship that God has prepared for us in imitation of Jesus, the full son of the Father. Only when our will coincides with the divine purpose can progress towards immortality be achieved. This immortality is something more than an endless succession of life in circumstances perhaps not very different from what we already know. It is, on the contrary, a state of resurrection in which we draw closer to God in thought and action while the physical universe transcends the limits of material existence to enter into a new relationship with eternity. As in Adam all men die, so in Christ all will be brought to life. This sentence of St Paul, already quoted, now takes on a heightened meaning. To be sure, when we ourselves die, our bodies are most unlikely to undergo the spiritualization demonstrated by the earthly remains of Jesus, even if we have attained great sanctity. It is only when mankind as a whole has attained such a state of sanctity that a bodily resurrection to spiritual eternity might be envisaged, and then indeed there will be no more death. Christ will be at hand then, for the Coming will be fulfilled.

What we are in process of achieving in this mortal life of ours at the present time is the fashioning of a spiritual body that will be our form when we have left the physical one behind us at the moment of our death. It returns to the earth from whose elements it was composed, but the immaterial mind/soul complex goes forth into the mental/psychic/spiritual realm clothed in a spiritual body whose elements are the thoughts and attitudes we manifested while we were engaged in earthly activity. As already noted, Jesus' spiritual body included his resurrected physical body, a circumstance outside our present competence. "What is sown in the earth as a perishable thing is raised imperishable. Sown in humiliation, it is raised in glory; sown in weakness, it is raised in power; sown as an animal body, it is raised as a spiritual body" (1 Corinthians 15:42–44). I believe that, in considering St Paul's wonderful exposition of the life beyond death, it is important to see that we create our own spiritual body. Indeed, it is our ultimate creation in this life, for everything else finds its fulfilment in it. The glory of the world passes away as we grow old, but what we have within ourselves grows even with the humiliating impotence of senility. This spiritual body is the wedding garment that a guest at the heavenly banquet lacked in the remarkable parable of Matthew 22: 1–14 with special reference to verses 11–14.

In the course of this account of creation we have

covered much ground: the universe, its earthly components and creatures culminating in the human, his own development from humble beginnings to the sophisticated people we now are, especially in the developed countries, and the human interaction with nature. We have found that only as we move from selfish acquisitiveness to world service can we be really fulfilled as people, for then we come fully of age and are no longer diverted by things to the exclusion of people. In other words, the *I-It* relationship of the uninstructed which ends in death has progressively to be replaced by the *I-Thou* relationship of deep personal commitment that finds its end in love. This love must extend beyond human relationships to the world of nature and ultimately all that is created, including inanimate objects. It is not a possessiveness that masquerades as concern, but such a burning identification with all that exists that one is prepared to give up one's very life for it. The accounts of those rare individuals who dedicated all their energy to conserving animal species that were on their way to extinction, which we considered in a previous chapter, are excellent examples of this love that is the basis of the higher creativity that alone can save our planet for the time of its resurrection. So also are those brave people who initiated hospices to care for the terminally ill, who previously were dismissed to care for themselves, non-productive members of society and therefore a mere burden on a community racing for money and power. That we all have something to learn from the disabled is a lesson that comes hard until we too have suffered. The same applies to the mentally ill as well as those born so handicapped that they will never become independent members of the community. All who have striven for their care have played their part in recreating the world in something of the image of God seen in the form of his suffering son who is both servant and Lord.

I find the words of Dietrich Bonhoeffer of great help, "To be a Christian does not mean to be religious in a particular way, to cultivate some particular form of asceticism (as a sinner, a penitent or a saint), but to be a man. It is not some religious act which makes a Christian what he is, but participation in the suffering of God in the life of the world." When we have attained that stature we are real people. Our spiritual body is well formed within us, and blessings flow from us to the world, which is gradually transfigured by our presence.

# Also available in Fount Paperbacks

## BOOKS BY C. S. LEWIS

### The Abolition of Man

'It is the most perfectly reasoned defence of Natural Law (Morality) I have ever seen, or believe to exist.'

*Walter Hooper*

### Mere Christianity

'He has a quite unique power for making theology an attractive, exciting and fascinating quest.'

*Times Literary Supplement*

### God in the Dock

'This little book . . . consists of some brilliant pieces . . . This is just the kind of book to place into the hands of an intellectual doubter . . . It has been an unalloyed pleasure to read.'

*Marcus Beverley, Christian Herald*

### The Great Divorce

'Mr Lewis has a rare talent for expressing spiritual truth in fresh and striking imagery and with uncanny acumen . . . it contains many flashes of deep insight and exposures of popular fallacies.'

*Church Times*

# BOOKS BY WILLIAM JOHNSTON

## Silent Music

A brilliant synthesis which joins traditional religious insights with the discoveries of modern science to provide a complete picture of mysticism – its techniques and stages, its mental and physical aspects, its dangers, and its consequences.

## The Inner Eye of Love

"This is a lucid comparison and exposition of eastern and western mysticism, from Zen to the Cloud of Unknowing, which can do nothing but good all round."

*Gerald Priestland, The Universe*

## The Mirror Mind

"William Johnston continues his first-hand studies of Zen meditation and Christian prayer . . . At his disposal he has had a twofold large and demanding literature. His use of it can be startlingly luminous."

*Bernard Lonegan*

## The Wounded Stag

This book examines the Old and New Testaments, the Christian mystical tradition, the Eucharist and mystical prayer, and explains how these can lead to the resolution of the conflict within men's hearts. A book with a message for today.

# Fount Paperbacks

Fount is one of the leading paperback publishers of religious books and below are some of its recent titles.

- ☐ FRIENDSHIP WITH GOD  David Hope  £2.95
- ☐ THE DARK FACE OF REALITY  Martin Israel  £2.95
- ☐ LIVING WITH CONTRADICTION  Esther de Waal  £2.95
- ☐ FROM EAST TO WEST  Brigid Marlin  £3.95
- ☐ GUIDE TO THE HERE AND HEREAFTER
  Lionel Blue/Jonathan Magonet  £4.50
- ☐ CHRISTIAN ENGLAND (1 Vol)  David Edwards  £10.95
- ☐ MASTERING SADHANA  Carlos Valles  £3.95
- ☐ THE GREAT GOD ROBBERY  George Carey  £2.95
- ☐ CALLED TO ACTION  Fran Beckett  £2.95
- ☐ TENSIONS  Harry Williams  £2.50
- ☐ CONVERSION  Malcolm Muggeridge  £2.95
- ☐ INVISIBLE NETWORK  Frank Wright  £2.95
- ☐ THE DANCE OF LOVE  Stephen Verney  £3.95
- ☐ THANK YOU, PADRE  Joan Clifford  £2.50
- ☐ LIGHT AND LIFE  Grazyna Sikorska  £2.95
- ☐ CELEBRATION  Margaret Spufford  £2.95
- ☐ GOODNIGHT LORD  Georgette Butcher  £2.95
- ☐ GROWING OLDER  Una Kroll  £2.95

All Fount Paperbacks are available at your bookshop or newsagent, or they can be ordered by post from Fount Paperbacks, Cash Sales Department, G.P.O. Box 29, Douglas, Isle of Man. Please send purchase price plus 22p per book, maximum postage £3. Customers outside the UK send purchase price, plus 22p per book. Cheque, postal order or money order. No currency.

NAME (Block letters) _____

ADDRESS_____

_____

_____

While every effort is made to keep prices low, it is sometimes necessary to increase them at short notice. Fount Paperbacks reserve the right to show new retail prices on covers which may differ from those previously advertised in the text or elsewhere.